I0815788

JANICE THOMPSON

Everyday Inspiration for Teen Girls

100 ENCOURAGING DEVOTIONS

BARBOUR PUBLISHING

Print ISBN 979-8-89151-151-4

Published by Barbour Publishing, Inc., 1810 Barbour Drive, Uhrichsville, Ohio 44683, www.barbourbooks.com

Our mission is to inspire the world with the life-changing message of the Bible.

Printed in China.

Introduction

The ups. The downs. The all-arounds. Life is tough. And navigating the teen years? Even tougher! You need all the help you can get, don't you? Whether you're celebrating victories or struggling through a rough season, you'll find something in this book just for you.

In the following pages, you'll find one hundred fun and engaging devotions on all sorts of topics you deal with daily—popularity, doubt, social media, stress, self-image, and so much more! The goal? To encourage you to spend more time in your heavenly Father's presence.

These inspiring devotions will give you that extra "oomph" you need to make it through your day. And guess what? The next one hundred days are going to be an adventure for you, girl! Seriously! Stick with it and you'll see a payoff. You'll come out of this season stronger, more encouraged, and ready to face whatever life throws your way.

Day 1

Popular

Yet there were many Jewish leaders who believed in Jesus, but because they feared the Pharisees they kept it secret, so they wouldn't be ostracized by the assembly of the Jews. For they loved the glory that men could give them rather than the glory that came from God!

JOHN 12:42–43 TPT

You try not to think about it. It's so dumb. Why does it even matter who likes who? Who's in? Who's out? I mean, really? Who makes up those rules, anyway?

And yet you find yourself struggling at times, wishing you could fit in. Those other girls? They have their cliques. They stick close together. They laugh. They gossip. They speak their own private language.

And it's bugging you. Oh, you don't mean for it to. But the way they completely ignore you when you walk by? Yeah, it hurts. You wish it didn't, but it does.

So what can you do about it? Force your way into their circle? Make them like you? Bend over backward to be like them so you fit?

Um, no.

Let's face it—no matter how hard you try, you can't force a piece into a puzzle when it doesn't really go there. And what would be the point of squeezing into that spot if it's not one that God intended for you? (Sounds painful, right?)

Think about the word *popular*. A popular person is widely liked. She's appreciated. People want her around.

Let's think this through: Aren't there people in your world who appreciate you even if you don't change yourself at all? Don't you have friends and loved ones who enjoy your company already? Surely there are friends, neighbors, siblings, or people at your church who think you're pretty special. Here's the point: You're already popular with the people who matter.

Want to know the best news of all? Jesus wants you. He's dying to hang out with you. (Literally.) You don't have to change a thing about yourself to be accepted by Him. He won't ignore you when you walk by, and He won't talk about you behind your back. He's the best sort of friend to have!

And He gets how you're feeling right now. People ignored Him too. A lot of religious leaders in His day refused to follow after Him because they were too worried about how it would make them look. Sound familiar?

So, yeah. He gets it. And He gets you. And He loves you all the same.

I'm popular with You, Jesus.
You want me, and that's enough! Amen.

Day 2

Without a Doubt

But when [Peter] realized how high the waves were, he became frightened and started to sink. "Save me, Lord!" he cried out. Jesus immediately stretched out his hand and lifted him up and said, "What little faith you have! Why would you let doubt win?" And the very moment they both stepped into the boat, the raging wind ceased.

MATTHEW 14:30–32 TPT

"Why would you let doubt win?"

Think about those words Jesus spoke to Peter just after his near-drowning incident. Do they seem a little harsh? (Hey, we all have doubts, right? Is God looking for perfection?) Maybe there was a little bit more to the story. Let's unpack it a bit.

Jesus had a long day of teaching and praying for people. He told the disciples to get into their boat and go to the opposite side of the lake. Then He went off by Himself to pray. (Side note: When you've had a long day and you're totally peopled out, sometimes the best thing you can do is hang out with God, just the two of you.)

Meanwhile, back on the boat, high winds blew up and tossed the disciples back and forth. In the middle of the chaos, Jesus came walking toward them—on the water.

Yep. You read that right. Feet touching down on the waves like they were a sidewalk. Like that was the most common, ordinary thing to do. He took step after step, coming right toward them.

The disciples thought He was a ghost. (Can you imagine how relieved they must have been to find out it was actually Jesus?)

Peter—a disciple who had pretty strong faith—decided he wanted to play copycat. He said, "Hey, Lord, if it's really You, call out to me and I'll walk to You!" Jesus called out to him, and Peter stepped out of the boat onto the water. (Don't try this at home!) As long as Peter kept his eyes on Jesus, he did okay; but the minute he looked away, he started to go down.

Here's the point, and you probably already get it: You'll go through rough seasons. One minute everything will be fine, and the next a big storm will blow in. You might feel like panicking. You might lose your faith. But it's during those times that you *really* need to keep your focus on Jesus. (No, really!) That's the only way you'll be able to keep from sinking.

Don't doubt. Just keep your eyes locked on His. And (no kidding) you'll witness miracles too!

Sometimes I feel like I'm sinking, Jesus. I'm so glad You're teaching me how to walk on water. I won't doubt. Amen.

Day 3

Under Pressure

Whenever I am anxious and worried,
you comfort me and make me glad.

PSALM 94:19 GNT

Have you ever filled a balloon with so much air that you thought it might pop? All it would take was a fingernail bumping up against it, and—*pow!*—it would blow up in your face.

Some days are like that balloon. They're so full of chaos and confusion that you can't think straight. Your anxiety is off the charts. And the day just gets worse as it goes along. You fail a math test. Your best friend gets offended about something. Your parents are angry because you didn't follow through on something you promised you'd do.

Yeah. Stuff can pile up.

Madison had a day like that. It started when her alarm didn't go off. She got to school late. When she arrived, she had a nagging headache that wouldn't quit. Then she realized she'd left her math homework at home.

In all the chaos, she forgot to pack a lunch. And there was no money on her account in the school cafeteria, so she ended up going without. Then, just about the time she thought the day couldn't possibly get any worse—pop quiz! Yep, her history teacher decided the class should have a surprise test on the one chapter she'd totally forgotten to read from their latest history assignment.

By the time she got home that afternoon, Madison was done. She just wanted to go to her room and crash. Unfortunately, her father decided this would be the perfect day to deep-clean the garage. She had an allergic reaction to all of the dust and ended up coughing and sneezing. She definitely didn't feel like doing more homework but had no choice.

Maybe you've had days like that. Your balloon is so full, you wonder how you'll survive. Fortunately, those "terrible, horrible, no-good" days are rare (in theory, anyway). Most days are just normal. So take the bad ones in stride. Don't overreact or you'll make yourself even more stressed out. (Hey, you know it's true!)

And remember, Jesus knows what it's like to face pressure. He certainly understands what it's like to have a rough day. He went through the roughest of rough days when He went to the cross for you. And guess what? He'd do it all again, hard or not.

I get so stressed out some days, Jesus!
I really feel like a balloon that's about ready to pop. On those horrible days, please show me how to take a deep breath and calm down. Amen.

Day 4

First on the List

Ask the Lord to bless your plans, and you will be successful in carrying them out.

Proverbs 16:3 GNT

"Girl, you need to get your priorities straight!"

How many times have you heard those words? It's not always easy to keep the most important things at the top of your to-do list, is it? Some days you just want to do what you want to do. Forget all of the things you're "supposed" to do. You can mess with those later. Right?

Unfortunately, when you skip over things on the important list, you usually end up paying a price. When the clothes don't get washed, you have nothing to wear. When you stop doing your homework, your grades slide. When you don't clean your room, you trip over things. When you forget to pray, you grow distant from God.

You get the idea.

Emma got the idea too. She was on track to graduate near the top of her class. At some point along the way, she stopped taking things so seriously. The internal decision was made to cut herself some slack, to let some things go. Sure, she still hoped to get into a great college, but maybe she wouldn't have to work so hard to get there. Maybe she could hang out more with her friends and have a better social life. That was important too.

Before long her grades were slipping. Sure, she enjoyed the parties, the extra time with her group of friends. They had a blast. However, there was a price to pay. She didn't get the scholarship she'd always counted on. In fact, she barely made it into the college of her dreams and had to take on a job and student loans to cover the cost of the tuition.

Little decisions today can have big consequences tomorrow. Of course, God wants you to have fun. He wants you to spend time with your friends. But keep everything in balance so that tomorrow isn't overwhelmed with things that should have been done today. Do that laundry. Wash those dishes. Do that homework. Do your best to keep healthy relationships. Pick up the stuff that's cluttering your room. You'll never be sorry tomorrow for the things you got done today.

I get it, Lord. I don't always put the first things first. Like hanging out with You, for instance. And taking care of the things You've given me to take care of. I get sloppy. I forget. I want to do my own thing. Thanks for the reminder that these things matter to You. Help me, please. Amen.

Day 5

One Is the Loneliest Number

"Be strong and courageous. Don't tremble! Don't be afraid of them! The Lord *your God is the one who is going with you. He won't abandon you or leave you."*

Deuteronomy 31:6 GW

It stinks to be left out. Knowing that you've been pushed to the side while others are included? Yeah, it hurts.

Isabella knew this feeling well. In eighth grade she was part of a great circle of friends. Then her family moved to a new school district. She started ninth grade knowing no one. The first few weeks stunk. Most of the other girls were already in close friend groups, and a lot of them didn't want to make room for one more.

She didn't push it. Isabella pretty much kept to herself and did her own thing. Sure, she would hear the other girls talking about hanging out at the mall or going to the movies, but she was never included. What was the point of trying to force her way in? Awkward.

Maybe you've been there. You're an Isabella. You wonder if you're completely invisible. Will they ever see you? Will they ever include you?

God designed you to live in community. That's why it hurts when you're pushed to the fringes. But there is a solution. You can begin to look for others like yourself who don't have a group. Make a point of seeing them. Notice them. Include them. Care for them. You can be the one with eyes wide open—the one who creates community for others. And you can have a blast doing it.

Sure, it means you'll have to be brave. And yes, you'll have to step out of your comfort zone. But remember, God is the one who gave you the desire to be with people. And because He created you, He knows you best. He can help you as you figure out how to connect with exactly the right people.

And since we're talking about God, remember: He wants to be included in the group too. Make Him the center of your friend circle. If you're truly feeling lonely, draw close to Him; and then ask for godly friends who can help you grow in your faith. He wants that for you, you know.

Thank You for being my best friend, Jesus. I'll never have to be lonely as long as I stay connected to You. My eyes are wide open. Show me others who need a friend. Make me brave as I reach out to them. Amen.

Day 6

Not a Normal Girl

I praise you, for I am fearfully and wonderfully made. Wonderful are your works; my soul knows it very well.

Psalm 139:14 ESV

You're not like the other girls. You don't dress like them, talk like them, or even think like them. You're not interested in the same things they're interested in. In fact, you think most of the stuff they worry about is really dumb. (Really? Why do they have to spend sooo much time gossiping and talking about who's crushing on who?)

Sometimes, though, you wonder if there's something wrong with you. Why did God make you so different? Does He want you to stick out like a sore thumb?

Here's a little-known fact: All girls feel different. No, it's true. Most don't feel like they fit in. So, to prove to themselves and others that they *are* normal, many of them overcompensate by hyper-focusing on the things they *think* "normal" teen girls care most about: popularity, makeup, hair, and guys.

Yeah, guys. We went there.

A lot of teen girls hyper-focus on their relationship with guys, thinking that's what a "normal" girl should do. But let's get real: There are a lot of things to think about when you're a teenager, other than just the opposite sex. Like school, for instance. And sports. And church stuff. And your family. And what you want to be when you grow up.

Alexis was one of the girls who felt different from the others. She had big plans to go far with her gymnastics and spent several days a week at the gym practicing her skills. She wasn't really into hair and makeup. Most days her hair was pulled up in a ponytail. And yeah, guys were great, but right now they weren't the number one thing on her mind. (Though, there was that one guy at the gym who caught her eye every now and again.) She didn't really have time for all that right now, though. She was focused on other things.

And maybe you are too. That doesn't make you weird or different.

But then again, what's so bad about being different? God created you to be unique, after all. So don't worry about trying to be normal. You just do you, girl.

Thanks for the reminder that different is okay, Jesus. I won't try too hard to look, act, or talk like the other girls. I want to be the best version of me that I can possibly be. Thanks for creating me to be unique! Amen.

Day 7

I'm Committed!

"A man who makes a vow to the Lord or makes a pledge under oath must never break it. He must do exactly what he said he would do."

Numbers 30:2 NLT

What does it mean to be committed to something?

Chloe had to face this question when she started figure skating lessons in her elementary years. She stuck with it for a few years and got better and better. She learned many amazing skills and met some great people. She formed a friendship with her coach and developed good social skills. Everything was going great. But by the time she got to eighth grade, her heart really wasn't in it anymore. She still showed up for lessons, but she didn't try as hard. Before long, she finally gave up. It just wasn't as much fun anymore.

It's one thing to give up a sport; it's another thing to give up on the big stuff—like relationships and academics and. . .God.

Yes, some girls give up on God. When things don't go the way they want them to, they drop Him like a hot potato. They don't stay committed.

A commitment is kind of like a wedding vow. When you commit to something (like promising to clean your room, for example), you're saying, "I will, no matter what." Only the "no matter what" part doesn't always play out the way you think it will. You get distracted. You get a better offer. ("Hey! Let's go to the mall!") You decide tomorrow would be a better day to complete the promised task.

But you promised. You committed. And once you start breaking commitments, they get easier and easier to break. Before long, no one really believes you when you say things like "Sure, I'll come to that Bible study group on Thursday morning before school," because they know you're probably going to send a text at the last minute saying you overslept.

The only way to remain committed is to start with the most important commitment of all—giving your heart to Jesus. Don't give up on Him. If you do, everything else will be ten times—no, a *hundred* times—harder. Stick with Him, and He will give you the tools to manage all of the rest.

I get it, Jesus! If I say I'm going to do something, I should do it. Please help me be more committed to the things I need to do. Amen.

Day 8

Yesterday Is Gone

No, dear brothers, I am still not all I should be,
but I am bringing all my energies to bear on this one
thing: Forgetting the past and looking forward to
what lies ahead, I strain to reach the end of the race
and receive the prize for which God is calling us up to
heaven because of what Christ Jesus did for us.

PHILIPPIANS 3:13–14 TLB

Olivia had a tough time letting go of things. Oh, not just hurtful things people had said and done, but also the bad things she'd done. The embarrassing things. The "I sure wish I hadn't done that!" things. She would replay them over and over in her mind like a movie clip. And even though she would try to push those negative memories away, they wouldn't go.

Like that horrible thing she said to her best friend. Or that snippy comment she made to her mom three days ago. Or that really awful time she cheated on a test. She prayed about these things but just couldn't seem to let go, no matter how hard she tried. And boy, did she try.

Here's the thing: When you keep something tightly clutched in your fist, there's no room left in your hand for the good stuff God wants to give you. There's an old fable about a little boy who was starving. He clutched crumbs in his hand and refused to let them go. The king sent yummy food, but the boy was so scared to open his hand that he starved to death, never realizing all he could have had.

Don't allow yourself to starve spiritually, girl. Open your hand. Let go of yesterday. It's filled with icky crumbs. They aren't providing you any nourishment at all. Not a bit. When you release them, God can begin the work of forgiving, restoring, and nurturing you with what you really need, His grace.

Maybe you don't feel worthy of grace. That's okay. None of us are. But He loves us all so much that He's willing to give it, even when we don't deserve it. That's the kind of awesome God we serve! There's always something better with Him!

It's not going to be easy, Jesus, but please show me how to let go! I know You have things that are so much better in store, but I can't have them until I release what I'm clutching in my fist. So here I go! Amen.

Day 9

Superstar!

In all the work you are doing, work the best you can. Work as if you were doing it for the Lord, not for people.

Colossians 3:23 NCV

You want to be a superstar. Okay, maybe not a superstar, but you'd love it if someone would notice your talents and abilities. Maybe brag on your singing voice. Talk about your amazing ability to hold an audience captive with your storytelling technique. Bring up that last game, when you got a great hit out into center field.

But people don't seem to notice the things you do well. (Or the things you *think* you do well.) They're too busy hyper-focusing on the uber-talented people out there. The girl who got the lead in the spring show. The gymnast who made state. The ballplayer who has aspirations of going pro. The class valedictorian.

And then there's little ole you. Trying hard. Working to get better at what you do. Practicing your French horn, hoping you'll make regionals. Developing your dance skills so that you can audition for the Christmas ballet. Working out every morning so that you'll be stronger for the upcoming softball season.

It's easy to feel overlooked or like your talents don't measure up. *(Hello? Did anyone notice that amazing roundoff double back handspring I just did?)* These days people show their support by sharing photos and videos on social media, and no one seems to be splashing your picture out there.

Hannah knew what it felt like to be overlooked and underutilized. She auditioned for a play at a local community theater and was placed in the chorus. Same thing for the next show. And the next. Meanwhile, she took an acting class and grew more confident. It took a lot of time—and she almost gave up—but her hard work eventually paid off. She got a big speaking role.

Your hard work will pay off too. But you can't give up. (I know, I know—you're tempted.) Keep at it. Don't give in to the temptation to quit when things get hard. And for pity's sake, don't compare yourself to others. There will always be someone better at what you do. Instead, focus on your own journey and leave the rest up to God. He has big plans for you, girl!

I'll keep working hard, Lord.
Thanks for the reminder that giving
up isn't the best answer! Amen.

Day 10

Focus!

Let your eyes look directly forward,
and your gaze be straight before you.

Proverbs 4:25 ESV

You know what it's like. You're supposed to be cleaning your room. You decide to start in your closet. You open box #1 and notice some old notes in there from a friend you hardly get to see these days. You get distracted reading them. Before you know it, you're on your phone, texting her. This leads to a decision to meet up for a movie. After the movie, you grab a bite to eat. After that, you end up talking for two hours to get caught up. By the time you get home, you realize you never tackled that messy room of yours.

Focusing on one thing at a time isn't easy these days! Life is filled with distractions. Notifications on your phone can keep you hopping. Texts. Social media. Phone calls. You name it, the ding-ding-dinging can make you crazy.

So how are you supposed to get anything done? That science project, for instance? Or those lines you're supposed to memorize for the drama class presentation? Every time you sit down to work, something gets in the way. Your focus shifts.

Cadence struggled a lot with her focus. From the time she

was little, ADHD was an issue. Her mom would tell people that Cadence was the poster child for attention deficit disorder. And Mom wasn't too far off with that description. Sitting still in class? Impossible. Focusing on what the teacher was saying? Grueling. Now, as a teen, the struggle to keep up with everything on her to-do list was overwhelming too. Between her classes at school, her messy room, and her church-related obligations, she was constantly frazzled. After a while, she got so overwhelmed that she just wanted to quit—all of it. Only, she couldn't quit school, so she had to stick with it, painful or not.

Maybe you can relate. So many things are calling your name that you don't know which direction to look. So your focus skips around—from school to home to church to sports to friends to social media. . .and back to school again. Then, by the end of the day, you realize you've overlooked a dozen things that should have been done.

Here's a little secret, girl: *Focus on Jesus first.* No, really. Go to Him first thing in the morning and ask for His help. He can help you prioritize so that you know what to do and when. He's pretty good at focusing. After all, He always has His gaze on you.

I'm coming to You, Jesus! Too many things are pulling at me. Help me to stay focused, I pray. Amen.

Day 11

Mental Health

Each time [the Lord] said, "My grace is all you need. My power works best in weakness." So now I am glad to boast about my weaknesses, so that the power of Christ can work through me.

2 Corinthians 12:9 NLT

Bailey struggled. A lot. If you asked her, "What's the main thing you're concerned about?" she wouldn't even know where to begin. She worried about her thoughts. They were all over the place. She felt twisted up inside sometimes and wondered if there was something wrong with her. One day she was up; the next she was down. There was no telling how she might respond to the next situation life tossed her way.

More often than not, Bailey battled depression. She couldn't really put her finger on why. Nothing specific was going wrong. Yes, she had some hidden fears. But why did she always feel down? Why was getting out of bed a challenge? Simple things like showering, getting dressed, and heading off to school each day felt huge to her. Overwhelming, even. And she stopped paying attention to her food choices, only eating when she felt like it. And she didn't feel like it very often.

Maybe you can relate to Bailey's struggles. These days

your mind is in a constant whirl. You can't seem to control your thoughts. You wonder if there's something wrong. Depression has settled over you like a dark cloud, and you wish you could shake it.

Many people struggle with these things but are afraid to voice them. It's important that you come clean and let someone know what you're dealing with. Why? Because things will only get better if you acknowledge them and bring them into the light.

Think about a pile of dirty clothes shoved under your bed. Will they ever get washed? Only if you bring them out into the light and deal with them. That's how it is with internal struggles. As hard as it might be, you have to reach down deep for the courage to say, "I need help," and then go to someone who will guide you toward the help you need. It might be a parent, an older sibling, a teacher, or a trusted friend. It might be a youth group leader or a pastor. But choose someone who will actually guide you, pray for you, and give you the encouragement you need.

There's nothing shameful in asking for help. We all need it from time to time.

Okay, I'm ready to bring things into the light, Jesus. But I'm definitely going to need Your help! Amen.

Day 12

Upside-Down World

Do not be conformed to this world, but be transformed by the renewal of your mind, that by testing you may discern what is the will of God, what is good and acceptable and perfect.

ROMANS 12:2 ESV

This world is messed up. And guess what? There are people out there who enjoy it this way. They want you to believe that what's wrong is actually right and what's right is actually wrong. And, if you speak up for truth—especially if it's a controversial truth—you'll be canceled. Written off. Left without friends.

But will you really? God will never leave you, after all; and He's your very best friend. And there are plenty of people out there who feel the way you do. They stand for truth. They don't give up. They don't give in to the temptation to flip their beliefs upside-down.

Here's the thing: There's power in numbers. So, instead of worrying about what other people think about your biblical values and beliefs, just buddy up with people who will pray for you. People who will stand alongside you.

Now, does this mean you have to lecture all of the people with different beliefs? Um, no. Live a godly life in front of them and lead by example. Go on loving all people, regardless of who they are, how they live, or what they do. But don't—and this is important—*don't* give in to the temptation to feel like you have to go along with the crowd. What if the crowd is wrong? Then what? Just because a ton of people all believe the same thing doesn't mean that thing is right. (Hello? Anyone remember the Holocaust?)

The Bible has answers for (literally) every issue going on in our twenty-first-century world. People don't want to hear what God's Word says because then they'll have to change their thinking and their actions. But His Word is true, and it never changes. (Check out today's verse.) So, if the Bible isn't changing, what is? Society, right? And it will go on changing. Today's "truths" will be tomorrow's lies. Ten years from now, there will be a completely different narrative.

That's why you have to know the truth, girl. The real truth. The whole truth. The truth that will save your soul and the souls of people you care about.

Don't be like the wind, shifting to every new belief system. Stick with the one thing that never changes—the Word of God. Only it has the power to transform lives. Amen?

Help me to live right-side up in this upside-down world, Jesus! Amen.

Day 13

The Gift of Problems

I am convinced that any suffering we endure is less than nothing compared to the magnitude of glory that is about to be unveiled within us.

Romans 8:18 TPT

Paige had problems. Lots of problems. From the time she was a little girl, she struggled academically. Then, in third grade, she got sick. At first no one knew what was going on. It took a while for the doctor to make a diagnosis of anemia. She changed her diet, but things didn't get much better, so she had to go for regular infusions.

Then, when she was thirteen, Paige's dad lost his job. The family had to move to a smaller house in a different school district. All of the friends she'd made at school were gone, just like that. And then the academic issues started. Good grief.

She sometimes wondered if she was a magnet for problems.

Maybe you feel like that too. You've faced more than your fair share of troubles—everything from health to financial to academic difficulties. Maybe you have to work harder than everyone else you know to get by in school. Or maybe your family has been hard-hit with sickness. It stinks.

But, on the other hand, blessings can come from problems.

Don't believe it? Let's go back to Paige for a minute. That smaller house she moved to? Her family ended up meeting some great neighbors who invited them over for a barbecue. The neighbor's company was hiring, and before long Paige's dad was hired and given a great new position. Oh, and those infusions she had to have at the hospital? Somewhere along the way, Paige decided she wanted to be a nurse when she got older. So the experience of being a patient led her to a life decision that would eventually help lots of other people.

God can take anything—literally, *anything*—and work it out for good. The biggest problem you face today (whatever that might be) is nothing but an opportunity for your heavenly Father. So don't give in to the temptation to throw your hands in the air and give up. Don't say, "Woe is me! My life stinks!" It might feel like it stinks right now, but God can turn it into a thing of beauty.

I'm ready for You to turn some things around, Jesus! My problems really get to me at times, and I need Your help to see them as opportunities. Amen.

Day 14

A Broken Heart

The Lord is close to the brokenhearted,
and he saves those whose spirits have been crushed.

Psalm 34:18 NCV

Has your heart ever been broken? Maybe someone you trusted said or did something that wrecked you. You couldn't believe it. Their actions really knocked the wind out of your sails. How could they betray you like that? You trusted them with your heart, and they took advantage of it.

Or, maybe someone you loved passed away unexpectedly. It was like a kick in the gut. She was too young! How could God allow such a horrific thing to happen? Wasn't He supposed to be loving? He could have stopped that accident from happening but didn't. Why? You have so many questions but can't wade through them because your heart is just so broken.

You didn't think you would ever get past the grief, nor did you want to. You'd never experienced anything like it, in fact. It was so painful that you felt it. Physically. In your heart. In your stomach. It messed you up. You couldn't even go through the motions of living normally again. Who could, with their heart shattered in a thousand pieces?

There's a reason they call it a "broken heart." These

horrible experiences affect us physically, emotionally, psychologically, and sometimes even spiritually. We often freeze in place, unable to move forward until healing comes.

But healing can come. Hearts really do heal. Ask any new bride about an old boyfriend, and she'll just smile and say, "I'm so glad that didn't work out!" She's already forgotten about the pain of the breakup. And talk to any woman who has remarried after losing a spouse. She somehow made it through the grieving process and moved forward into a new, hopeful relationship.

God wants you to move forward too. Yes, you'll need time to grieve. This is natural and completely acceptable. But don't allow your fragile, broken heart to rule you for long. Pray for healing, and it will surely come—in God's time and God's way. Give yourself room to mourn; but then trust that the one who knows you best and loves you most will turn your ashes into a thing of great beauty. He will, if you allow Him to.

You can take my broken heart and mend it, Jesus. I know it might take time to get past the pain, but I give my heart to You today. Begin to work in me, I pray. Amen.

Day 15

The Helpers

Do your best to present yourself to God as a tried-and-true worker who isn't ashamed to teach the word of truth correctly.

2 Timothy 2:15 GW

"Look for the helpers."

Maybe you've heard that phrase but wondered what it meant.

The helpers are the ones who stick around to do the dirty work after everyone else leaves. They're passing out papers at school, assisting the coach on the ball field, supporting a friend who is going through a scary cancer diagnosis.

They're sweeping up crumbs, baking cookies, and sewing costumes for friends in the big show (the same show in which they weren't given a part).

Helpers hold the world together. Tasks would never get done without them. You wouldn't be where you are without them! (Someone had to feed and clothe you.) The helpers are like the glue, holding the other pieces in place. They don't need to be in the spotlight. They don't have to get the applause. They're perfectly happy to serve. To encourage. To mend. To support.

Maybe you're a helper. You have that desire inside of your

heart to be an encouragement to others. Emily knew what that felt like. As a little girl, she was the one the teacher called on to help with tasks in the classroom. She was always happy to be of service.

Later she became so skilled at organizing things that people started calling on her to help whenever they had a big event. She would come and work behind the scenes, pulling things together—setting up tables, organizing the food, helping with the paperwork. Anything that was needed. She never minded. Feeling helpful brought her great joy.

Maybe it brings you joy too. Girl, it should, because you were created in the image of a holy God who gave and gave and gave some more! He was (and is) the greatest helper of all. And He put that desire to help others in your heart. So look for ways to do that today. Who is struggling and needing a kind word? Who could benefit from a plate of home-baked cookies? Who could use a quick "I'm here if you need me" text?

Helpers might not get the applause, but all of heaven stands and cheers when they sweep in to save the day. And, hey, what's better? The applause of your peers or the applause of heaven? (Hint: If you said heaven, you would be right.)

Go forth and help, girl! What are you waiting for?

Thank You for the helpers in my world, Lord. Help me to be one too. Amen.

Day 16

Growing and Changing

When I was a child, my speech, feelings, and thinking were all those of a child; now that I am an adult, I have no more use for childish ways.

1 Corinthians 13:11 GNT

Some girls want to grow up *waaay* too fast. They start thinking about makeup, boys, dating—all of that stuff—way too soon. Other girls, though? They wish they didn't have to grow up. They're perfectly content with things the way they are. Can't life just stay the same forever?

Mackenzie fell into that category. She was perfectly happy just hanging out with her family, letting her parents make all the decisions. When she got to her late teens, they encouraged her to step out and look for a job. She wasn't keen on that idea. It sounded frightening to her. In fact, a lot of things sounded frightening. And when they suggested she start looking into colleges, Mackenzie got completely overwhelmed. Leave home? Move to a dorm? That didn't sound appealing at all. Wasn't there a local community college she could consider? Would that work? What did it really matter, anyway?

No matter which category you fall into, growing up can be daunting. Whether you want to fly the coop right now or stay at home forever, one thing is inevitable: Time will pass. You will get older. Things will change. And you will have to change with them. (Hint: This is true whether you stay home or eventually move away.)

Here's some good news: Even though your situation will take twists and turns, God will never change. Throughout the whole process—on good days and scary ones too—He'll be exactly the same as He was yesterday. His Spirit will be just as real, just as powerful. He'll still speak to your heart and give you direction. He won't leave you or forsake you. He's going to stick with you, even when you're unsure which way to go.

So no matter where you go or what you do, you can count on Jesus going along for the ride. In fact, He's the one driving the car! And if you've learned one thing, it's this: You can trust His GPS system! So don't be afraid to grow up. Embrace it. Learn from it. Enjoy it. And trust the one who created you, because He thinks that growing up is a terrific idea!

I'm putting my trust in You, Jesus! Thanks for driving the car. I'm always safe with You. Amen.

Day 17

Identity: Lost and Found

You are chosen people, a royal priesthood, a holy nation, people who belong to God. You were chosen to tell about the excellent qualities of God, who called you out of darkness into his marvelous light.

1 PETER 2:9 GW

Maybe you've heard the question "How do you identify yourself?" These days that's a loaded question.

The Bible asks the same question but with a different motivation. God wants to make sure you understand one often-forgotten truth: You are a child of the Most High God. You should identify as a child of the King. (Yep, you really are a princess!) Problem is, most people don't identify that way. They forget. They feel like they have no value. (Would a real princess ever feel this way? Never!)

God will never devalue you. Society will, but He won't. So begin to identify as a bold, confident child of the King. You'll firm up your faith as you proclaim it! And remember, you are created in His image. You're like Him in more ways than you know. You can identify as one who is created in the image of her Creator!

Aubrey struggled with knowing how to identify. For years she was "the pastor's daughter." (Her dad was the pastor of their church, after all.) Some people knew her as "Gina's daughter." (Hey, her mom was pretty popular and always surrounded by people at the church.) Then, for a while she became "Jenny's sister." (Jenny had some time in the spotlight during the years she led the youth group's worship team.) People sometimes identified Aubrey by who she hung out with: Leesa's friend. Bobby's neighbor. Mary's classmate. Mrs. Johnson's student.

It bugged her. She wanted something to set herself apart. But she wasn't "known" as anything special. Then, one year at church camp, a counselor got through to her. She helped Aubrey see the light. As a believer, Aubrey was a daughter of the Most High God! Her identity was in Him.

Your identity is in Him too! So stand up straight! Walk tall! Never forget who you are and *whose* you are! There. Doesn't that make you feel special?

Thank You for reminding me that my identity is in You, Jesus! Sure, I'm somebody's daughter, somebody's friend, and somebody's student. But most of all, I'm Your daughter! Amen.

Day 18

Grumpy Gus

Do everything without complaining or arguing. Then you will be blameless and innocent. You will be God's children without any faults among people who are crooked and corrupt. You will shine like stars among them in the world.

PHILIPPIANS 2:14–15 GW

Emilia was what her dad called a "Grumpy Gus." She just couldn't seem to help herself. Whining, complaining, making a big deal out of things—that was her go-to. Most days she was moody and couldn't seem to help it. Everything irritated her. The way her sister looked at her. The assignments her biology teacher gave the class. The way the other girls at school interacted. The sound of her brother's laugh. Everything. And she always seemed to be in a bad mood, even on days when there was no reason to be.

Maybe you know an Emilia. Maybe you are an Emilia. You just can't seem to rise above the whining and complaining, no matter how hard you try. (Hello? Are you trying?) It's easy to find the flaws in people—and situations—when that's all you're looking for. Some people excel at finding the bad. They're experts at it, in fact. (Would you happen to fall into that category, perhaps?)

Maybe you're a Negative Nancy. A complainer. A faultfinder. And your behavior is having an effect on you. People are pulling away. You're not a lot of fun to be around, and they're picking up on it. The chronic complaining is getting old, even to you.

So how do you break this cycle? Maybe it's as easy as printing up today's verse and taping it to your bathroom mirror.

"Do *everything* without complaining or arguing." Let's start right there. Jesus isn't asking. He's telling. He's commanding. And, honestly? *Everything* really means, well, everything—schoolwork, chores, relationship challenges—*all* of it.

"Then you will be blameless and innocent." Well, ouch. That one hurts! It's hard to consider yourself blameless when you're part of the problem, after all. Sure, you don't really consider yourself to be part of the problem; but if whining and complaining break God's heart, then maybe it's time to reevaluate.

Here's the point: You don't have to go on being a Grumpy Gus forever. You can rise above the need to find the negative. You really can. You'll find great freedom on the other side of it too!

C'mon, Emilia, you can do this.

I'm sorry, Jesus. I don't mean to be so negative or moody. I don't mean to see only the faults in people. Help me turn this around, I pray. Amen.

Day 19

Technology Whiz

So, then, brothers and sisters, don't let anyone move you off the foundation of your faith. Always excel in the work you do for the Lord. You know that the hard work you do for the Lord is not pointless.

1 CORINTHIANS 15:58 GW

Reese was kind of a technology nerd. She loved all things electronic—from video games to phones to computers. She just seemed to have a knack for technology from the time she was little-bitty.

When the teacher needed someone to demonstrate something to the class, she called on technology-savvy Reese. She jumped into action—not to show off but because she felt confident she could handle it. And her talents weren't overlooked by her parents either. From the time she started showing an interest in these things, they encouraged her to learn all she could. After all, she could easily make a living working in the technology field. They realized the benefit and encouraged her skills.

Maybe you're drawn to technology too. You're a whiz at figuring things out and can't wait to try your hand at all of the latest, greatest electronics coming on the market. Maybe, when the pandemic hit, you were totally cool with doing school by computer. You thought it was great, in fact. And people called on you to set up the online chats. When something went wrong, they knew who to text. And you loved being able to help. What took others hours to figure out, you could do in minutes or even seconds.

Okay, so not everyone loves all things electronic. Could be you're one who struggles to figure all of that out. (You're the one who takes hours to figure out her lost password, perhaps.) And you're also aware of the dangers. After all, some big tech companies are trying to control what we see, hear, and believe. So we have to be careful when we start dabbling in technology too deeply or for too long.

That said, there's plenty of room in the technology field for Christians to make their mark. Remember, our ultimate goal is to spread the gospel, and technology can be a huge help as we seek to do that.

If you're feeling the pull, learn all you can. But remember to put your faith at the forefront. You'll face temptations to do things the world's way. Don't go there. Use the tool of technology to help others come to know Jesus. What a lovely mark you'll leave on the world if you choose to do that.

I'm ready to take on the world, Jesus! Okay, not the whole world, just the technology part of it. Guard my heart and protect me as I learn all I can so that I can reach others for You. Amen.

Day 20

Has Anyone Seen My Motivation?

Put God in charge of your work,
then what you've planned will take place.

Proverbs 16:3 msg

Bella's motivation was lacking. She didn't feel like doing anything today. Pulling the covers over her head and sleeping another couple of hours sounded great.

But Mom had other ideas. Today her mother wanted to do what she called "spring cleaning." Ugh. That meant every corner of the house had to be scrubbed, mopped, or dusted. And the clutter in Bella's space—well, it was stacked pretty high.

So, yeah. Staying in bed sounded good but impossible. (Please, Mom? Don't you get it? I'm wiped out!)

Maybe you've struggled with motivation on busy days too. You'd rather not, thanks. That big project in your history class? Could you skip it? That upcoming math test? Could you opt out? That early morning exercise class you signed up for? You've had a change of heart. Nothing sounds good right now. And you have a thousand reasons why you can't possibly follow through.

Here's the problem—once you start making excuses, you'll

keep making them. And making them. And making them some more. Before long, they'll become a lifestyle. And let's face it, lazy adults usually got their start when they were younger. (There's no time like the present to address these feelings, in other words. You might as well get this over with, girl.)

So push back the covers. Ask God to give you the motivation and the energy. He will, you know. It comes from His Spirit. (By the way, the Spirit of God is where all of your energy comes from—on good days and bad.)

And here's a fun truth: The more you do, the more you feel like doing. It's true! Before long, you'll be like a snowball rolling downhill, picking up speed as you go. You'll have a clean bedroom, a tidy bathroom. And those cobwebs in the corners? They'll be gone too! Even the cat will thank you for giving her a clean litter box.

Out of bed! You have work to do.

Okay, I'll confess—I don't always feel motivated, Jesus. There are days (just keeping it real) when I just want to stay under the covers. Life is hard, I'm exhausted, and I deserve a day off, right? I'll do the right thing, even if it's hard. But I'm gonna need Your help! Amen.

Day 21

Risky Behavior

If we say that we have no sin, we deceive ourselves, and there is no truth in us. But if we confess our sins to God, he will keep his promise and do what is right: he will forgive us our sins and purify us from all our wrongdoing. If we say that we have not sinned, we make a liar out of God, and his word is not in us.

1 John 1:8–10 GNT

Adrianna liked to live on the edge. Sure, she called herself a Christian. Her family went to church. Sometimes. But she didn't really fit in with those kids. They were a bunch of fakes, anyway. So two-faced. Adrianna decided on a different sort of life. She'd pretend to be a Christian when she was at home, but at school and with her friends? Well, that was a whole different thing. There she could be herself—a brave, daring, crazy girl, willing to try just about anything. As long as the grown-ups weren't looking.

For a while, no one really suspected. But Adrianna started dabbling in some risky behaviors. It started with a guy she met at a party. Before long, they were texting. And, well, things got—shall we say—bad. She found herself doing and saying things the old Adrianna never would've done. And this guy, who seemed to captivate her thoughts, talked her into doing other risky behaviors—things like drinking and dabbling in drugs. Soon her heart was broken, her mind in a whirl, and her parents confused.

They still had no idea she was up to anything. She'd done a terrific job of playing the role of the good daughter. But they could tell something was off. She wasn't their old Adrianna anymore. And then, one day, she got caught. (Hey, your sin always finds you out, right?) At that point, she had no choice but to come clean.

Maybe you know an Adrianna. Maybe you *are* an Adrianna. You've dabbled in some things you shouldn't have. You know better. It feels wrong. You feel sick inside, actually. But you can't seem to stop that cycle. And there are plenty of people out there willing to talk you into doing even more risky stuff if you want to be part of their crowd.

So, here's an important question: What's it going to take to stop? No, really. What's it going to take to back away from the fire, to admit that the risky life isn't the life for you? What you need is supernatural courage, which can come only from God. It's time to face the truth and decide, once and for all, that you're going to be who you say you are.

I'm ready, God. Really, I am. I'm done with the old me. I'm done with risky behaviors. Help me break free, I pray. Amen.

Day 22

The Right Way

Another reason I wrote you was to see if you would stand the test and be obedient in everything.

2 Corinthians 2:9 NIV

Elizabeth liked to do things the right way. She became irritated when people didn't pay attention to the instructions, because those folks always made things harder than they needed to be. Like when she had to do that group project in her world history class and the others in the group seemed to have no idea what was expected of them. Or that time the family was invited to a white elephant gift exchange and her mom thought it was a normal gift exchange.

Elizabeth paid attention, and it irked her when others didn't. The world would be a better place if people just did things the right way.

Maybe you're like Elizabeth. You're a stickler for doing things a certain way. You don't like to waste time. Or energy. "Do it once and do it right" is your motto. And it drives you crazy to see people try to shortcut or make up their own rules. *Why couldn't they just follow the instructions? Don't they get it? Instructions are there for a reason. Duh!*

Or, maybe you're the opposite. You have to put together a

new scooter and you toss the instructions aside. Or you help your mom put up the artificial Christmas tree, but it ends up with the branches in all the wrong spots. Maybe you open a box of cake mix and toss in a little oil but don't measure it. Maybe you add one egg and figure out later you were supposed to add three. Oops.

Instructions are important. Doing things the right way really does save time in the end. (Hey, if you've ever had to take something apart and put it back together the right way, you know that's true.)

The same can be said of your faith walk. You can choose to follow the instructions in the Bible, to do things the right way. If you do, you'll have an easier, calmer life. Or you can go your own way and try to shortcut God's plan. In the end, you'll pay a big price. His ways are higher, after all. And His instruction manual? It's the best! He didn't skip one detail!

So what's it gonna be, girl? Are you going to play by the rules or make things harder on yourself? Do it the right way (His way), and you'll never be sorry.

Okay, I'm ready to do it Your way, God!
I'm going to read the instruction manual and
figure out this faith thing once and for all. Amen.

Day 23

Believe for It

"Whatever you ask in prayer, believe that you have received it, and it will be yours."

Mark 11:24 ESV

Maybe you've heard a TV preacher shout, "Just believe for it!" You wonder if he's lost his marbles. Just believing for something will actually make it happen?

Yes. And no.

God does long to give you the desires of your heart, and His Word promises that an effective prayer will be answered. But it's important to pray according to His will. In other words, you can't just randomly pray for a motorcycle for Christmas. Well, you could, but you might be disappointed if the "just believe!" mantra didn't work. You might end up with a completely different gift, but it will probably be just what you need—not necessarily what you want.

See, God desires the very best for you. But He also wants to increase your faith. So, if you take the time to get to know His heart and His Word, you'll be more likely to pray things like "God, please help my parents cover the mortgage this month" or "I need peace in that weird relationship I'm in at school."

The Lord is really good at showing off in situations like

these. He loves to prove Himself and does so time and time again—from the time we're young until we're very old. He's always tickled when He can say yes to your prayers.

Faith learned this the hard way when she turned sixteen. She was hoping—no, praying—that her dad would get her a new car. Unfortunately, that didn't happen. She ended up sharing her brother's old clunker.

But over time, she started to appreciate it more because she realized how hard her brother was working to make the payments. After a while, she decided to do something fun to help him, so she raised the money to pay off the balance.

Man, it felt good! And God reminded her that His plan all along was a lot more exciting than her own.

So go ahead. Ask in faith. And "just believe!" But do so with a humble heart, ready to admit that God's way is always the best way. And remember, if He does say no, it's always because He has something much better in mind.

I get it, Jesus. My prayers have to be sensible! Show me how to pray according to Your will, and then increase my faith. Amen.

Day 24

Agreement Prayer

"Again I tell you this: If two of you agree on earth about anything you pray for, it will be done for you by My Father in heaven. For where two or three are gathered together in My name, there I am with them."

MATTHEW 18:19–20 NLV

Have you ever heard the term "agreement prayer"? It's when two or more people come together and agree to pray about the same thing. They link arms (symbolically or sometimes even physically) to make a difference. There's power in numbers, for sure!

And there's something kind of special about agreement. (If you've ever been in a *dis*agreement, you know how awkward that can be!) When you agree with someone, you're on the same page. You're a team. (Picture a football team all agreeing on the same play. It's like that, only ten billion times more powerful.)

The Bible says that if two or more of you agree on earth about anything you pray for, it will be done for you in heaven. That's a powerful promise! So maybe it's time to gather the troops. Link arms. Be like a Red Rover team, a long invincible line the enemy can't penetrate. Then, from a position of strength, link your prayers together for the big stuff—your sick grandmother; your parents' upcoming divorce; your father's anger problems; your brother's drug addiction.

Cassidy discovered the power of agreement prayer when her dad was in the hospital with cancer. She asked her friends to pray. And the youth group leaders. And her teachers at school. Anyone who would listen to her. She even asked the elderly lady down the street to pray.

Everyone linked arms and prayed until Cassidy's father finally recovered. It took awhile—and there were some rocky moments—but knowing that others were praying helped get her through. In fact, Cassidy counted on those prayers. They gave her great strength during the moments when she started to feel scared.

You can ask for prayer warriors to link arms with you too. Don't go it alone, girl. You were never meant to. Grab a like-minded Christian friend and get her on board. Then watch as God intervenes on your behalf.

Thank You for the reminder that I don't have to do this by myself, Lord! Show me who to ask. I need some strong prayer warriors for the things I'm facing! Amen.

Day 25

Big Deal or Small Deal?

We don't look for things that can be seen but for things that can't be seen. Things that can be seen are only temporary. But things that can't be seen last forever.

2 CORINTHIANS 4:18 GW

Brooke blew everything out of proportion. Like, *everything*. If her mom asked her to do the dishes, she argued until her mother finally gave up and said, "Forget it." If someone hurt her feelings, she made it a really big deal and refused to forgive or to forget about it. When she got a little cold, she acted like she was dying. In short, she was a little extra.

Maybe you know someone like Brooke. (Hey, maybe *you* are like Brooke!) Some people make big deals out of small ones. They see obstacles as mountains. They view ordinary relational problems as breakup material. They overreact to, well, everything.

So how do you stop that sort of mentality? Maybe to you everything *is* a big deal. Maybe every disagreement seems like a fight. Maybe every sniffle feels like strep throat. Maybe every bad grade feels like you're not going to get into the college you want to go to.

There's really only one way to get past this, girl. It comes down to the word *perspective*. You have to keep everything in perspective.

Until now, maybe you've been viewing everything through your "big deal" filter. It's time to change that filter and use the one God gave you. He says that most stuff is temporal—not eternal. It's really not going to matter when this life is over.

So keep that bad grade in perspective. Begin to view your obstacles as what they are—bumps in the road. They're not insurmountable hurdles. They're not unbreakable walls. They're just bumps. And simmer down when you're upset at someone. It's not the end of the world when your parents ask you to do something around the house. In fact, as a Christian, it should be part of your makeup to "do unto others what you would have them do unto you" without even having to be asked.

Perspective. It's a filter that's going to make everything better.

Okay, okay, I'll admit it. Sometimes I overreact, Lord. I make huge deals out of small ones. I act like the world's coming to an end when it's really just a speed bump ahead. Help me see things the way You do. I want Your perspective! Amen.

Day 26

Bake Yourself Happy

Eat honey, dear child—it's good for you—
and delicacies that melt in your mouth. Likewise
knowledge, and wisdom for your soul—get that and
your future's secured, your hope is on solid rock.

PROVERBS 24:13–14 MSG

Peyton loved to bake. Whenever she felt down in the dumps or had a bad day, she would head to the kitchen to try out a new recipe. People all over the neighborhood loved her baking days, because they ended up with her cookies, pies, scones, and cupcakes. And while she mixed, mixed, mixed the eggs, butter, and sugar, she was really working out her worries of the day, letting them go. *Ah, that felt good!* (And the desserts she cooked up tasted pretty good too!)

Before long, Peyton learned a lot about the process of baking and even created some of her own concoctions. Her recipes were yummy. The cookies tasted divine, and the cakes looked almost professional. She wasn't really trying to make a career out of it; but by the time she got to high school, Peyton wondered if maybe she should. Maybe she could run her own bakery someday. Or go to culinary school.

Maybe you're like Peyton. Baking is great therapy for you.

When you've had a stressful day, mixing up butter, sugar, and eggs is just the ticket. And you love blessing others with the yummy treats you make. Nothing wrong with that!

It's fun to turn your bad day into a good one by distracting yourself. Whether you do it with a bubble bath, baking, or a game of cards with your kid sister, there is always a way to process your troubles. And it's good not to get hung up on the bad stuff, after all.

So enjoy your time in the kitchen. Whip up some sweet treats, and share them with your loved ones. You'll learn a lot about the sweetness of God as you give your problems over to Him.

I love the distraction of baking, Lord.
It's kind of fun to forget my troubles and
mix up a batch of chocolate chip cookies.
Or snickerdoodles. Or a yummy cake. Or brownies.
You get the idea! I love sweets. And by the
way, thanks for always being so sweet to me.
I'm grateful for Your kindness to me. Amen.

Day 27

Courage, Girl!

"Be strong and courageous. Do not be afraid or terrified because of them, for the Lord *your God goes with you; he will never leave you nor forsake you."*

Deuteronomy 31:6 NIV

Being brave isn't always easy. Sure, they make bravery look like a piece of cake in the movies. Superheroes jump into action and save the day. They conquer their fears in no time at all. In real life, though? Your hands shake. Your knees knock. Your voice quivers. You turn to mush when you have to step outside your comfort zone.

Gabrielle knew that feeling well. Her mother signed her up for piano lessons. She loved playing, but as that first recital was announced, she thought she might throw up. Finally, the big night arrived. Somehow she made it up onto the stage. But when she sat on the piano bench, her hands were shaking so hard that she couldn't calm down long enough to find the right keys. And when she put her foot on the pedal, it started bobbing up and down. She drew in a deep breath and got started. A few notes fumbled, but she made it through. Thank goodness. But she would *never* do that again!

Maybe you're like Gabrielle. The idea of performing in

front of people terrifies you. So you don't. You just hide your light under a bushel. Oh, you don't mind practicing privately. But in front of a crowd? No thanks. You'll just skip that part.

Here's the thing, though. God didn't give you those abilities so that you could hide them. The point of having abilities is to spread His love, His life, to others. It's a fun way to do evangelism (to spread the gospel). When you're hiding in your closet, that's hard to do.

So face those fears, girl! Whether you're performing or simply giving a presentation in school in front of your classmates, step out of your comfort zone. Do the hard thing, even if your voice quivers. And guess what? The more you do it, the easier it gets. Really, it does. If you start now, by the time you're grown, you'll be standing in front of crowds with ease! So jump that hurdle. Be brave. And always remember where that courage comes from, anyway. It's straight from the heart of your Daddy God!

I'm so glad I can ask You for courage, Jesus! Sometimes I'm such a scaredy-cat. My knees knock and my hands shake. Then You enter the picture, and I'm suddenly filled with supernatural courage. I need that today, Lord! Amen.

Day 28

A Million Little Miracles (They're All around You)

You are the God who works wonders; you have made known your might among the peoples.

PSALM 77:14 ESV

Mia was always on the lookout for miracles. She seemed to find them everywhere. Things that others would call coincidences, she always called God's tiny wonders. Her eyes were opened to the miraculous at every turn—whether she was at home, at work, or at play.

Once you start looking for miracles, you'll surely find them. In the face of a newborn. In a litter of cuddly puppies. In the intricacies of the human body. In the variety of flowers in your grandmother's garden. In a rainbow after a storm. In the patterns of snowflakes on a frosty day. In the moon, hovering over the earth below and offering light to guide the way. In twinkling stars that shimmer and shine in dazzling display against the dark night sky.

There are a million little miracles on this planet (and beyond), and they're all around you right now. Don't believe it? Oh, girl! You just don't know what you're missing! Maybe you just need to change how you view things!

Think about it this way: You witnessed one very important miracle when you woke up this morning and put your feet on the floor. You, girl, are a miracle! You're a living, breathing creation, filled with wonder and imagination. You witnessed another as you ate your breakfast. How miraculous to know that God provided food for your body to thrive (and your parents could afford to buy it). And that drive to school? It was a miracle that kid on the bike didn't get hit by your mom's car. He came pretty close, after all.

And yet he was fine. Another miracle.

When you're looking for them, these moments miraculously appear. (Funny, how that happens, right?) God's tiny wonders are (literally) everywhere. But we have to open our eyes to see them, don't we? We have to say, "Jesus, give me Your eyes to see and Your ears to hear. I don't want to miss a thing!"

So what's keeping you? If you seek, you will surely find! Your God is a God of miracles, after all.

I'm going to keep my eyes wide open, Jesus. I know miracles are all around me. I want to notice them. I want to thank You for them. Even now, I'm thinking of two. No, three! No, a thousand! Thanks for doing miracles, Lord. Amen.

Day 29

Leave Me Alone, Please!

After [Jesus] had dismissed the crowds,
he went up on the mountain by himself to pray.
When evening came, he was there alone.

MATTHEW 14:23 ESV

Brianna was peopled out. She couldn't take any more—of their conversation, their arguing, their music, their. . .*everything*.

So she hid out in her room. In fact, if she had her way, she'd spend even more time in here, far away from the chaos and confusion. Here she could have peace. Here she could have quiet. Here she could have rest.

Her parents weren't thrilled with the idea of Brianna pulling away for too long, so they kept bugging her to come out and join the family for movie night or game night or other "fun" things that just didn't seem like fun to her right now. Really? Hanging out with a good book and the cat sounded a lot more relaxing and enjoyable.

Maybe you're a Brianna. You're more comfortable in your own space. Sure, you can handle people—to a point. But then you have to have some peace and quiet. It's just how you're wired. Don't they understand?

It's fine to pull away when you need to regroup or chill. And it's also good to enjoy your own company (be comfortable alone). And Jesus led by example: He pulled away from the crowd for some alone time with His Father. These moments energized Him for the work ahead.

Same with you. But remember, God made you to live in community, so don't pull away forever. Those people who annoy you? The loud ones? The crazy ones? They're still part of your circle, and you're meant to enjoy their company. It might take some work, sure. (Doesn't it sound funny, thinking you'd have to "work" to enjoy being around people?) But they are worth it.

And remember, for every introvert, there's an extrovert. There's a girl who is just the opposite of you. If you told her to go to her room alone, even with the cat, she'd lose her mind. "What would I do in there?" she might cry out.

Isn't it funny how God made us all so different? But He's creative like that, and He enjoys every single personality type. Just one more reason why it's important to gather with others from time to time—so you can experience them all yourself!

Okay, okay, I get it. Too much alone time isn't really for the best. Show me how to live my life in a balanced way so I don't get overwhelmed, Jesus. Amen.

Day 30

Keep Your Spirit Strong

Let Christ's word with all its wisdom and richness live in you. Use psalms, hymns, and spiritual songs to teach and instruct yourselves about God's kindness. Sing to God in your hearts.

COLOSSIANS 3:16 GW

Jade's family was really into health. Her mom only purchased organic foods and made sure the kids didn't have soda or too much sugar in their diets. They were uber-careful about things like preservatives and stayed away from processed stuff as much as possible. And boy, did they ever believe in supplements. In fact, her mother sold them to everyone she met.

Health meant a lot to the family, and it didn't just stop with physical health. As a strong Christian, her dad knew the value of making sure the whole family was in tip-top spiritual health too. He took this very seriously. So, like lots of other people, they went to church together on the weekends. And sometimes midweek too. But Dad took it further than that. He held nightly Bible studies with the family before bed. Hardly a night went by when they didn't gather in the living room for prayer and praise time.

And, as Jade grew, she came to appreciate these times, because the prayers from her family members caused them to grow closer together. While many of her friends were pulling away from their moms and dads, the relationship with hers was only getting stronger.

Maybe this sounds like a pipe dream to you. You can't even imagine sitting around with your family, talking about the Bible or praying out loud. Impossible. Your family? They're nuts. They don't care about stuff like that. Or maybe they care, but they're just too busy. Or too messed up.

Girl, if that's the case, you can start a new tradition. Choose one sibling—a younger sister, maybe. Offer to do a quick devotion before school in the morning. Or pray with her before she goes to bed at night. Do everything you can to develop your own spiritual health and that of those around you as well.

And remember, those supplements you're taking? They're great! They boost your metabolism and give you energy. But the Bible? It's even better at boosting your spiritual metabolism and giving you all you need to get through the day. So dive into the Word of God. It will keep you healthy and strong.

I want to keep my spirit strong, Jesus.
Show me how I can do that and
help others I love too. Amen.

Day 31

High Expectations

Christ's message in all its richness must live in your hearts. Teach and instruct one another with all wisdom. Sing psalms, hymns, and sacred songs; sing to God with thanksgiving in your hearts.

Colossians 3:16 GNT

Lily was an ambitious girl. She had high expectations. From the time she was a little girl, she always wanted more—not *for* herself but *from* herself. Nothing she ever did was good enough. She strived for perfection. And boy, was she ever busy! Talk about a worker bee! Go, go, go. Push, push, push. That was Lily's style.

Many people called her "driven." (Hey, she was like a car barreling down the highway, sometimes.) Others would say, "She's performance-based," meaning she only felt good when she was performing some task.

But there was more to the story. For example, Lily was never okay with ordinary. *Extraordinary* was the word that propelled her every day. So she pushed her own boundaries (in a good way) so that she was always growing, always getting better at the things she did. Schoolwork. Grades. Artistic abilities. Sports. Relationships. Job-related things.

She wanted to be better, better, better.

And her hard work paid off. She did well in school and got the lead in the fall show. She got promoted at work and won awards in the Junior League. She raised money for fundraisers, helped her dad paint the living room, and even helped out at an inner-city mission during the holidays, feeding the poor.

But Lily noticed one thing she couldn't really confess to others: The better she got at something, the less she enjoyed it. Instead of singing or acting just for fun, it became more like a job. Everything became a task. And no matter how "good" she was at something, she always beat herself up after doing it. Nothing was ever good enough, at least to her way of thinking.

Maybe you've been there. You're a worker bee too. Here's the thing: Jesus wants you to do well, to have high expectations, but He doesn't want you to wear yourself out in the process. Oh, and that whole "not good enough" thing? Yeah, that has to go. In His eyes, you're doing a terrific job. So get back to loving what you do, girl. You'll be a blessing to yourself and others as long as you're having a blast doing what you've been called to do in this life. And remember to take a break from time to time. Remember: Even God took a day off! Amen?

**I get it, Jesus! High expectations are good—
to a point! Help me keep my life in balance. Amen.**

Day 32

Good Deed Doer

It is not given to you because you worked for it.
If you could work for it, you would be proud.

EPHESIANS 2:9 NLV

Remember that scene in *The Wizard of Oz* where the Wizard says that the Tin Man is a "good deed doer"? He explains that people with even the tiniest of hearts can do good things for others.

Maybe you're like that. You're a good deed doer. You're always on a quest to take care of others, to make sure they have what they need. And you're not content to do a little. Not you! You go above and beyond, making things extra special for them.

Here's the thing, though—no matter how hard you work, no matter how many good deeds you do, you can't save yourself. You could give money to the poor, travel to developing countries and feed the homeless, even take care of the sick, and it wouldn't earn you a ticket to heaven. There's only one way to get there, and that's through trusting in the sacrifice of Jesus on the cross.

Does this mean God doesn't want you to do good deeds? Oh, He definitely wants you to live this way. Good deeds are, well, good! Even though they can't save you, they shine a light on the Lord, which is a wonderful thing! And it makes your heart happy to bring a smile to others, doesn't it?

Lara gave her heart to Jesus when she was fourteen, and her eyes were opened even more to the needs around her! She wanted to save everyone. The friendless girl in history class. The family who didn't have food to eat. The poor man on the side of the road. The child with no shoes. The elderly woman down the street with no friends. She rallied on their behalf and did great deeds to help them. She loved and cared for them and shared the love of Jesus with them too.

While others walked right past someone, not worrying about their well-being, Lara always seemed to notice. She was a great lover of people and an inexhaustible caregiver. Knowing and loving Jesus made her heart bigger than ever before.

The same thing will happen for you. Give Jesus your heart. Let Him save you (definitely not something you can do for yourself). Then watch as He turns you into a people lover!

I get it, Lord. I didn't earn it. But that doesn't mean I can live any way I like. So I'll live for You! And in the meantime, I'll go right on doing good deeds for others. (It feels really good to help out!) Amen.

Day 33

Ticktock, Body Clock

Or do you not know that your body is a temple of the Holy Spirit within you, whom you have from God? You are not your own, for you were bought with a price. So glorify God in your body.

1 Corinthians 6:19–20 ESV

Samantha hated the mornings. Hated, hated, hated them. Every single morning, she groaned, hit the snooze button, and pulled the covers over her head for ten more minutes of sleep. Eventually she had no choice. She had to crawl out of bed. But, man. Those first few hours were rough. Okay, okay, if you asked her why, she would have to confess that she was up pretty late the night before. But, hey, who could blame her? Her body clock seemed to run that way. She was a night owl, after all. It truly felt like her body wanted to be awake in the night and asleep during the day. Thank goodness for Saturdays.

Maybe you can relate. You're a "stay up late" kind of girl. Those early mornings really get you down. You do your best work late at night. Homework? It's a lot easier at midnight than at 7:00 p.m.

Or maybe you're just the opposite. You spring out of bed at the crack of dawn, ready to go. You can't wait to face the day. But by four in the afternoon, you're wiped out. And by nine at night? Well, you're crawling in bed, grateful the day is behind you.

Every person is born with his or her own body clock. When you're in school (and/or have a job), you have no choice. You have to work with the schedule you're given. But it's hard for those who simply don't do mornings. They struggle to get going!

You can play tricks on yourself to adjust that clock. Start to wind down earlier. Drink chamomile tea in the evening. Stay away from caffeine after dinner. Take a warm bubble bath an hour before bedtime to relax. Train yourself to do what you have to do.

But, on the other hand, work with what God gave you. If your best work is done in the evening, then go for it! Don't try to do that homework at four in the afternoon if it feels impossible. Zip through it when you're raring to go.

You get the idea. God designed you to function the way you function. You'll figure out how to make the most of it if you rely on Him.

I'm figuring out my body clock, Lord!
Show me how to make the best of it.
Give me the strength I need to get everything
done in Your time and Your way. Amen.

Day 34

You Choose

Trust in the Lord with all your heart, and do not trust in your own understanding. Agree with Him in all your ways, and He will make your paths straight.

Proverbs 3:5–6 NLV

Alyssa had a hard time choosing. When her family went to lunch at a buffet, she stared at the foods but couldn't figure out what to order. It all looked great. She got overwhelmed trying to decide. The same happened every time she picked up a menu at their local Chinese restaurant, so she always ended up getting the very same thing. Boring!

And, man, did she ever have a hard time picking out a dress for that first homecoming dance. It took weeks of trying on dozens and dozens of pretty dresses before finding just the right one.

Choosing felt more like work. And she had that feeling of having to commit to something. What if she changed her mind afterward? Then what? Could she take the dress back and trade it in? Sounded complicated. So she opted to buy nothing at all. Then the day of the dance came, and she ended up borrowing a dress from her older sister, one that didn't even fit right. Ugh.

Maybe you get it. You're not good at choosing either. You've struggled to choose the right friends. And the right foods. And the right classes to take. You can't make up your mind when it's time to buy a new outfit or choose a friend group. So you freeze in place like Alyssa did.

Life will offer you a zillion opportunities to choose, but there's one choice you can make that's more important than any other.

Choose to respond to Jesus' call on your life.

Choose to give Him your heart. If you haven't already done so, choose to make Him your Lord and Savior. Choose to keep walking with Him, even when it gets hard. Choose to say yes to the things that bring Him joy and no to the things that break His heart. And choose to love others with His love, even the people who make doing so really, really hard.

That might sound like a lot of different choices, but it really starts with one: Choose Jesus. If you choose Him and put Him first in your life, every other choice you make will be easy. He'll make it easy. Why? Because He adores you, girl.

I choose You, Jesus! And while I'm at it,
show me how to make good daily choices—
with my food, my activities, my relationships,
my studies, and everything else too! Amen.

Day 35

Girly-Girl

Charm is deceptive, and beauty does not last; but a woman who fears the Lord will be greatly praised.

Proverbs 31:30 NLT

Amber came out of the womb loving all things girly. Frilly dresses. Fancy shoes. Tutus. Glitter. Pink decor. You name it—the girlier the better. Fluffy, curly, swirly, girlie—yes, please! She begged to have her ears pierced when she was in first grade. The "pretty princess" costume? Yeah, she had to have that too. With matching shoes. And crown.

When she hit her teens, Amber turned her attention to hair, makeup, and pretty clothes. These things came naturally to her. She wasn't in it to get attention. In fact, she just really, really loved the process and the outcome. But, man! She got good at it. Before long, others were coming to her for fashion advice. She just had a knack for making things look great.

Her older sister, Julia, though? Yeah, she was just the opposite. A pair of jeans and a hoodie were just fine with her. She yanked her messy hair up into a ponytail most days and didn't give a second's thought to it after that. Some days she put on lip gloss, but that was only to keep her lips from getting chapped. She couldn't care less about the things Amber enjoyed. She was totally comfortable with her way of doing things and oblivious to the thoughts of others.

Talk about two different approaches to beauty. And yet both girls were equally pretty in their own ways. And they got along well with each other in spite of their differences. In fact, they grew to appreciate those differences, even laughing about them at times.

Here's the thing: The Bible makes it clear that you don't have to rely on the trappings of this world to be beautiful. You're created in the image of God, after all; and He's the most beautiful of all. And you don't want to be vain (turn the attention on yourself). That's not God's way either. You're supposed to let His light shine, not your own. But that doesn't mean you have to give up on the fun stuff.

Go ahead and be yourself. If you want to be frilly, go for it. Want to scale things back? Enjoy! Don't let the pressures of this world convince you that you need to conform. Enjoy your natural tendencies, and use them as part of your daily beauty routine.

Thanks for the reminder that You find
me beautiful, no matter what, Jesus!
I don't have to rely on external beauty
to be gorgeous in Your sight. Amen.

Day 36

Contentment

Not that I am speaking of being in need, for I have learned in whatever situation I am to be content. I know how to be brought low, and I know how to abound. In any and every circumstance, I have learned the secret of facing plenty and hunger, abundance and need. I can do all things through him who strengthens me.

PHILIPPIANS 4:11–13 ESV

Where is your contentment level? If you had a meter to gauge your contentment, what would it look like? (Hey, some days are great and you're totally content. Other days? Not so much!) You wish you could be more content, but with life swirling around you, it feels totally impossible. And that's the problem, right there: feelings.

So how do you deal with them? Or, rather, how do you get beyond them? Here's a hint: Have you ever watched a baby sleeping in his mother's arms? He's not stressed about something that happened ten minutes ago. He's not anxious about tomorrow. He's completely content, at peace in the safety of those arms wrapped around him. As long as he's close to the one who knows him best and cares about him most, he knows he's safe. And safety brings immediate feelings of contentment.

We have a lot to learn from babies. When they're left alone in a crib, they cry. But when they're held close, their fears vanish. Their worries disappear. There, in the embrace of their mother or father, they feel safe, valued, cherished, and totally at peace. They learn, in small snippets, how to brave the "alone" times because of how secure they feel when they have physical contact with Mom or Dad.

That's the way it should be when you spend time with Jesus, girl. No matter what you're facing in your day-to-day life, you can be content in Him. Let Him hold you close. Allow Him to help you work through what you're thinking—and feeling. And remember, as you step out into the scary stuff, you'll learn how to be content even then if you recognize how deeply you are loved by your heavenly Father.

He's as close as you will allow Him to be. So draw close today, girl!

Okay, Jesus, I get it. You want my nearness. It's not enough to talk about You. I have to talk with You. And spend time with You. Only then will I find the safety, security, and contentment I need to face the scary stuff. Thanks for the reminder. Amen.

Day 37

On-Screen Violence

Do not envy a man of violence and
do not choose any of his ways.

Proverbs 3:31 ESV

Arianna loved her TV shows. She was addicted to a ton of them. Some nights she barely slept. She just had to watch that next episode. On and on she went, getting deeper and deeper into the plot. What would happen next? She would have to stay awake to find out.

At first some of the shows shocked her a little. The language was, well, rough. But more and more, she found herself thinking, *Aw, it's okay. It's not real, anyway.* So she justified it. She made excuses, saying things like "It's just entertainment, a way to pass the time."

She felt the same way about violence in the shows she watched. Instead of worrying about it, she actually thought it was exciting. Before long, she started watching more and more shows with violence in them.

Then she noticed something kind of odd. She was angrier than before. She couldn't seem to help herself. Her temper reached the out-of-control point. She found herself acting more like the characters in her show.

Maybe you can relate. You're prone to watch violence in shows. Like anything else, if you have a steady diet of it, you'll pay a price in the end. (Think of what it would be like if you only ate candy and nothing else.) That's kind of what it's like when you hyper-focus on one type of entertainment and drink it in like water. Before long, you'll pay a price. Your thoughts will change. Your level of tolerance will change. You'll start justifying things you didn't justify before.

So shy away from those not-so-great shows, girl. You know you should, anyway. And remember, there are other ways to pass the time. Like baking cookies for that family in need. Or hanging out with your siblings. Or taking the dog for a walk.

You get the idea. Get out there! Do something active, and leave those TV shows and movies where they belong—on the back burner.

Lord, I am sorry for the way I've given myself over to some of the TV series and movies. They're so much a part of me that I hardly notice the bad stuff anymore. Make my spirit more sensitive to the things that break Your heart. I don't want to do (or watch) anything that would make You sad. I'm going to need Your help, for sure! Amen.

Day 38

Self-Harm

I can do all things through Christ who strengthens me.

PHILIPPIANS 4:13 NKJV

If you've been paying attention to the struggles of your fellow students, no doubt you've run across a troubling problem, one that seems shocking to you. Some people are into what doctors call "self-harm." They cut themselves. Or starve themselves. Or turn to drugs or alcohol. Or think of other ways to physically punish themselves or ease some sort of internal pain they are going through.

Maybe you've experienced feelings like this yourself. If you have, there is hope. You can stop. It won't happen on your own; but with God's help, you can turn this thing around. Please don't give up.

Eva started feeling the "need" to cut her arms when she was in seventh grade. The family had just moved to a new school district, and she didn't know anyone. Loneliness was getting to her. Then, at her lowest point, her parents decided to split up. So there she was, in a place she didn't even want to be, and her dad walked out the door. Terrific.

So she tried to ease the pain by causing even more pain. It didn't help, of course. And it also didn't take long for someone—a girl in her math class—to notice. She told the teacher. Eva was angry. At first. But after the school counselor got involved, Eva found herself in weekly sessions with a therapist.

And those sessions helped. A lot. She eventually got control of this part of her life.

If you've reacted to stress by doing something dangerous—throwing up your food, cutting yourself, or any other sort of self-harm, consider this little devotion a message straight from God to you. He wants you to stop. He needs you to stop. And He's going to give you a way to stop. It starts with sharing your struggle with someone and adding the words "I need help." Then, when help arrives, take it. Follow their instructions. Do the hard work to overcome this.

You can overcome this, you know. Take a close look at today's verse: You can do *all* things through Christ Jesus who gives you strength.

Yes, even this.

Jesus, my heart breaks for those who are struggling. I pray that You will sweep in and do what only You can do. Heal their hearts. Heal their minds. Be with them and bring total peace. Amen.

Day 39

Hold on to Me (When You Feel Like Giving Up)

Do not let yourselves get tired of doing good.
If we do not give up, we will get what is
coming to us at the right time.

GALATIANS 6:9 NLV

Have you ever heard that old saying "When you reach the end of your rope, tie a knot and hold on"? Well, maybe you're there now. You're done. Kaput. There's not one ounce of energy or "want to" left in you. Giving up is the only option.

Is it, though? God never intended for you to give up. Sure, He wants you to give in—to Him. See His outstretched arms? See His open palms? He's saying, "Take that problem and put it right here. I'll carry it for you, and your load will be easier." He's not just saying that. He really means it, with His whole heart. He loves you that much, girl!

Kayla knew what it felt like to give up. For weeks she tried and tried to pass her college-level physics class. No matter how hard she studied, she just couldn't get it. Her grades were slipping more with every single test. And when it came time to study for the final exam, she had a "What's the point, anyway?" attitude.

That's exactly the attitude Satan wants you to have during hard moments, by the way. If he can get you to say, "What's the point?" then you've completely lost your focus. He's a sly, tricky enemy, intent on bringing you down. Don't let him!

Kayla decided to give it one more push. She called a good friend who was doing well in physics, and they studied together. And, in the end, she got an 82 on the final, which was just enough to pull her grade up to a C for the course. Not ideal, but a whole lot better than failing.

Here's the point: The only way to truly fail is to stop. Read that again. The only way to truly fail is to quit. So don't quit. Keep going. And even if things don't turn out as you'd hoped, you'll never have the regret of saying, "I should've tried harder."

Try harder.

Keep pushing.

Lean on Jesus.

And don't ever, ever, ever give up.

I won't give up, Jesus. Thank You for the reminder that You're right here, ready to help. Give me the strength and the courage to keep going, even when I don't feel like it. Especially when I don't feel like it! Amen.

Day 40

Disrespect

Obey your leaders and submit to them, for they are keeping watch over your souls, as those who will have to give an account. Let them do this with joy and not with groaning, for that would be of no advantage to you.

HEBREWS 13:17 ESV

Kayla had a teensy-weensy problem. Her mouth. She couldn't seem to control it. Things were especially hard when an adult tried to tell her what to do. Who did they think they were, anyway? Didn't they see she was almost seventeen and old enough to make her own decisions? Honestly.

So she got a little "catty" in her responses. She smarted off. She rolled her eyes. She didn't take them seriously. And worst of all, she led by example, so her siblings and friends followed suit.

The adults in Kayla's life didn't take her behavior well. In fact, her over-the-top reactions definitely made things worse, not better. Things got particularly bad at home with her mom. Before long, they were barely speaking in normal tones to each other.

Kayla couldn't seem to stop, though. After a while, she became known for her attitude. Her teachers? Yeah, they saw it. And the principal? He figured it out quickly too. And her parents almost reached the point where they stopped trying. If not for a youth group leader's diligent work, Kayla never would have turned things around.

Here's the problem with lack of respect for authority. First of all, it breaks God's heart. Take a close look at today's verse. He put people over us for a reason, and we're called to humble ourselves and submit to their authority in our lives. It's not easy, but when we cool our jets, it's easier on everyone.

Second, when we begin to disrespect our elders, those God has placed over us, or even our friends, we're setting an example. We're saying, "Hey, everyone. Be like me. I get away with it."

And maybe you do get away with it. For now. But a day is coming when you won't. If you stop respecting those God has placed over you, it won't be long before your boss fires you—or worse.

So, yeah, examine your heart. Repent. Ask God to give you a different outlook—and a different mouth to speak more respectfully to others.

(Sigh.) I get it, Jesus. I need to guard my heart, my attitude, and my mouth. I'm definitely going to need Your help with this one! Amen.

Day 41

Just Enough and Just in Time

"Give us today our daily bread. And forgive us our debts, as we also have forgiven our debtors. And lead us not into temptation, but deliver us from the evil one."

Matthew 6:11–13 NIV

Abby was trying to raise money to go on a mission trip to Guatemala. For a while, it looked like the funds wouldn't come in. She needed over $1,200, and a week before the trip she only had $750. Then something miraculous occurred. She prayed, and God answered! Checks started arriving. People gave gifts anonymously. Her grandparents chipped in. Then her neighbor. Then her aunt from Wisconsin.

When the day arrived, she had everything she needed and more. Abby could hardly believe it! Then again, she had prayed that God would meet her need, and He did! (He loves to show off like that.) In fact, so much money came in that she was able to help another girl pay for her trip as well. Talk about a win-win!

Abby's story is exciting because it reminds us that God always gives what we need when we need it. Okay, so some-times He waits until the very last minute; but that's part of the faith journey, isn't it? In the end, He always, always, always comes through for us, making provision for the need. Maybe this is why Jesus told the disciples to pray, "Give us this day our daily bread." He could've said "our weekly bread" or "our monthly bread," but He didn't. He said *daily*. Why do you suppose that is?

Philippians 4:6–7 (ESV) promises, "Do not be anxious about anything, but in everything by prayer and supplication with thanksgiving let your requests be made known to God. And the peace of God, which surpasses all understanding, will guard your hearts and your minds in Christ Jesus."

We have to focus on today. Right here, right now, you have all you need. So don't get too keyed up, fretting over all of the things you think you need for tomorrow. Don't start with the "God's not going to pull through this time" stuff. He will. He always does. It might not look like you expect it to (He's good like that). No doubt, it will look better! And for sure, your faith will grow as you wait on Him. But, in the end, He'll give you just enough—and just in time.

Jesus, I know I can trust You! You're going to give me what I need when I need it. Thank You so much for Your faithfulness to me. Amen.

Day 42

Even at My Worst

I pray that Christ may live in your hearts by faith. I pray that you will be filled with love. I pray that you will be able to understand how wide and how long and how high and how deep His love is. I pray that you will know the love of Christ. His love goes beyond anything we can understand. I pray that you will be filled with God Himself.

EPHESIANS 3:17–19 NLV

Savannah had a rough day. Everything that could possibly go wrong did. It started that morning with the realization that her only jeans that fit since putting on a few pounds were dirty. Then came the part where she made her sister late for class. Then the argument she had with her best friend in the hallway outside of her English classroom. Ugh. It was an all-around terrible day. And her reaction to all of that? Well, she didn't handle it the way she should have. She certainly didn't exhibit Christlike behavior. Just the opposite, in fact.

That night when she crawled into bed, she got to thinking about some of the things she had said in anger. The way she had slammed her books down on the kitchen table. The attitude when her mother confronted her. The terrible things she'd said to her sister. The ugly text message she'd sent her best friend, blasting her for how much she supposedly hated her.

Her friend didn't hate her. Savannah knew that. But right now, wallowing in the icky feelings, she didn't exactly feel lovable. And Savannah even wondered if God still loved her after the horrible way she had behaved.

Maybe you've had a day like Savannah. Things got rocky, and you reacted in the worst possible way. Now you're feeling regretful. You can smooth things over with the people in your world, but does God think less of you?

Here's the truth, girl: You are His child. And all kids make mistakes. When your baby brother pitched a fit and knocked over the lamp, did your parents stop loving him? Of course not.

Neither will God stop loving you. Ever.

Even on the worst possible days.

It's been a rough day, Jesus. Then again, You already know that. You saw (and heard) everything. Please forgive me for the ugly things I said. Can I have a do-over? Please? And please show me how to make things right with my family and friends. I really want tomorrow to be better! Amen.

Day 43

An Attitude of Gratitude

Therefore let us be grateful for receiving a kingdom that cannot be shaken, and thus let us offer to God acceptable worship, with reverence and awe.

HEBREWS 12:28 ESV

"Have an attitude of gratitude."

No doubt you've heard those words and not just at Thanksgiving time. But what does it mean to live with a heart of gratitude? How does that play out in the real world? Are you supposed to go around saying "Thank you!" all day long?

Lauryn tried to figure it out. Her youth group leader gave the kids a challenge: Be grateful for everything.

"Everything?" she asked.

"Yes, everything," he responded.

Okay, then. She did her best to view everything differently, starting right away. When her mother washed her favorite jeans so she could wear them, Lauryn took the time to thank her, grateful for her mom's sacrifice. When her history teacher offered extra credit on a project, she thanked her too. When her grandfather offered to help her with her math homework, she baked him some cookies as a thank-you.

Every time something small happened, she saw it for what

it was—a gift. And every kind gesture—from the smile on the cafeteria lady's face to the trip her dad made to the store to buy a new charger for her phone—was seen as a gift too. (Hey, those things really are gifts, after all!)

Before long, her heart was overflowing. She truly saw—and appreciated—all that God was doing for her. And it made her want to do for others too. So she smiled at the cafeteria lady first. And she made the teacher's job easier by turning in assignments on time. She thanked her parents for their sacrifices, and she even (gasp!) went out of her way to treat her kid brother better.

Everything in Lauryn's life improved when her attitude changed.

Maybe this really resonates with you. You want to have an attitude of gratitude too. It's easy, girl! Just ask God to give you His vision so that you can see things the way He does! He wants you to realize that gifts are everywhere! So, eyes wide open!

Thank You for Your many gifts, Lord! And thanks for all of the amazing people You've put in my life. They are loving and giving, and I don't want to take any of them for granted. Show me how to bless them as they have blessed me. I want to be the best gift giver! Amen.

Day 44

Fight for What's Right

So Christ has truly set us free. Now make sure that you stay free, and don't get tied up again in slavery to the law.

Galatians 5:1 NLT

Have you ever met those people who seem defensive all the time? They're ready for a fight. It's like they have their fists up in the air every time you see them. Whoa. What's their problem, anyway?

It's one thing to be defensive about dumb things; but when it comes to defending God, that's another thing altogether! Believers need to get bolder and braver, ready to defend their faith and to defend the Lord. They have to be brave. They need more courage than ever, especially these days!

How does that play out? Maybe someone tells you that Christians don't have a right to believe what they believe. Um, wrong! Or maybe they say you shouldn't be able to worship the way you want to. Wrong again. You have a right (and an obligation) to worship. They might tell you to keep your mouth shut about political things, but that's not right either! Christians are supposed to make a difference in all areas of life, including politics.

Christians face other types of opposition too. Some of

their friends might say, "Your God can't really perform miracles." You sweep in with a great story about a time that He showed up big-time with a really cool miracle, like that one time when He healed your grandmother. Or that other time when your friend was in deep depression, but Jesus turned her situation around.

Here's the thing: There will always be people who think they know better than you. They even think they know better than God! (Wrong.) He's still the King of the universe, whether they believe it or not.

So be ready to share what you believe, along with actual stories of times He came through for you. (This is your testimony, by the way. And the Bible says that people will be won by the word of your testimony, so go on sharing your personal stories when the timing is right.) And don't back down when people say that you have to change something about your faith. You go right on standing, girl. Be brave. And you will change your world.

Thank You, Jesus, for courage to stand up for truth. I won't back down, no matter how difficult it gets. I want to be an example to others to be courageous too, but I'm definitely going to need Your help! Amen.

Day 45

Keep on Keeping On

Therefore, since we are surrounded by such a huge crowd of witnesses to the life of faith, let us strip off every weight that slows us down, especially the sin that so easily trips us up. And let us run with endurance the race God has set before us. We do this by keeping our eyes on Jesus, the champion who initiates and perfects our faith. Because of the joy awaiting him, he endured the cross, disregarding its shame. Now he is seated in the place of honor beside God's throne.

HEBREWS 12:1–2 NLT

Have you ever met anyone who started well but didn't finish? Maybe you have a friend who always has some crazy, over-the-top idea. She goes for it and takes off like a rocket aimed toward the moon. But then, about halfway into it, she changes her mind. Or gets tired. Or distracted. Off she goes in a completely different direction—just as motivated, but just as likely to fall short of the goal.

Brooklyn was like that. She thought it would be cool to become a photographer, so she begged her parents for a camera and other photography equipment. But after a while, she lost interest and the camera sat on a shelf. Maybe she could talk her parents into buying her a horse so she could join the equestrian team, she thought.

So what's up with all of these people who don't finish what they start? What does the Bible say about them? They're like runners in a race who take off out of the starting gate but get tangled up in the stuff in their path. They lose their perseverance. They get distracted by bright and shiny objects in their path. "Oh, look! Something else to get my attention!"

Don't get distracted. Keep on keeping on. In short, do what Jesus did. In spite of the pain, in spite of the way He was treated, He focused on "the joy awaiting Him." What joy, you ask? The joy of knowing that His sacrifice would buy your freedom and offer you eternal life with Him.

There's great joy ahead for you, girl! It will be worth the pain in the end, so don't give up. Keep on keeping on.

I won't give up, Jesus. I feel like it sometimes, but I want to be a girl who finishes well. The next time I'm tempted, please remind me that finishing the race is just as important as starting it! Amen.

Day 46

So That You Will Be Forgiven

"When you stand and pray, forgive anything you may have against anyone, so that your Father in heaven will forgive the wrongs you have done."

MARK 11:25 GNT

Aurora couldn't seem to let go of things. Months—or even years—after the fact, she would still replay the stories in her brain. That time her mother yelled at her. That time her so-called friend lied about her. That time her brother blamed her for something he did. She tried to forgive them but couldn't seem to let go.

For a long time, she thought it was her right to hang on to the bitterness she felt over these things. Then, after she gave her heart to Jesus, she kept stumbling over verses like today's verse from Mark 11:25 about forgiving in order to be forgiven. Ouch. Did God really expect her to forgive and let it go?

Let's face it, humans have a hard time forgetting. Even if you are able to forgive, pushing an incident out of your memory bank is next to impossible. But one thing is for sure—the more you replay the story in your mind, the longer you will hang on to that bitterness. The sooner you say, "Jesus, I'm putting this behind me," the sooner you will live in peace. And the only chance of making things right with the person who hurt you is if you truly let go.

You might wonder if that's a real thing. Can you pick up where you left off with the girl who lied about you? Can you trust your brother not to blame you again? Yes. And no. Some life experiences leave us sadder but wiser. That means your eyes are wide open from now on. But it doesn't mean you're jaded (or suspicious). It just means you live wisely.

Today, for your sake as well as for the sake of the person who hurt you, forgive. Go to Jesus and tell Him that you're ready to give it to Him. Sometimes it helps to write down the thing (and the name of the person) you're forgiving, then tear up the paper and flush it down the toilet. A physical demonstration will always remind you that you truly let it go.

It's not impossible. In fact, it's God best plan for moving forward.

Forgive. Today.

Jesus, it's not going to be easy, but today I choose to forgive ____________________ for the time he/she did this to me: ____________________. Help me to put it behind me, Lord. Amen.

Day 47

What Season Are You In?

For everything there is a season,
and a time for every matter under heaven.
ECCLESIASTES 3:1 ESV

Maybe you've heard the expression "Life moves in seasons." It's so true. Some are up; some are down. Some are good; some are bad. It's never easy to predict what season you'll be walking through next. But they are all doable with God on your side (even if they seem really, really hard).

Kaitlyn found this out the hard way. She was a social butterfly, always surrounded by friends, family, and neighbors. People naturally gravitated to her. But then the pandemic came and everything changed. She wasn't able to be around people much, and she became more of a homebody. Afterward it was kind of hard to pick up where she'd left off. People were still hesitant to get out, and she didn't really blame them.

In some ways, the pandemic was like a winter season. In the winter, things slow down. The grass stops growing. Everything is covered in snow and ice. Under the frozen ground, nothing springs to life.

But remember, after every winter—whether real or

psychological—comes spring. Things always bounce back. Life always springs forth. Trees produce leaves. Plants produce fruit. Grass grows.

And the things that have been dormant in your life—relationships, romance, job opportunities—spring back too.

Here's the thing: You can't "buck" the seasons. (Think of a horse trying to buck a rider off of his back.) When you fight the seasons, they're even harder to bear. So settle into whatever season you're in. Give it to God. Say, "Father, I trust You with this season I'm going through." Then watch as He gets you through it and then transitions you to another season. And then another. And then another.

Spring will come. Summer will come. And then autumn, forcing you to slow down and prepare for another winter. That's the cycle of life. But, girl, you can trust God, no matter what season you're walking through. And you'll learn a lot about yourself in how you respond to those changes too.

Thank You for the seasons, Jesus! I'm so glad it's not always winter. I'm always grateful for the spring and summer. But today I choose to praise You for all of the seasons, even the ones where I feel I'm not getting enough opportunities. I give those to You, Lord. Amen.

Day 48

Where Do You Stand?

Jesus Christ is the same yesterday and today and forever.

HEBREWS 13:8 ESV

Your friends are divided into two very different camps. One group believes one way. The other group believes the other way. You're torn. When you're with Group A, you can see their side of things. But when you're with Group B, they do a stellar job of proving Group A wrong—or so it seems. So you side with them.

The problem is, you don't seem to have a mind of your own. When you're completely alone, you're torn. You spend hours wrestling internally, going back and forth. What should you believe? Is there a way to come to the truth on your own?

Following after others is a problem, girl. Why? Because, what if both groups are wrong? Then what? If they're all wrong, then who's right? And how do you figure out the right way if you're not being led by others? Could it be that God's Word has a better answer—one you can find on your own—without asking others' opinions?

The only way you'll know for sure is to dig into the Bible and find out the answers for yourself. There's not one question you could ask—literally, not one—that you won't find the answer to in the Bible.

Questions about sexuality? They're in there. Questions about how to treat others, even if they're living in a way that isn't biblical? That's in there too. No matter the problem or controversy, the Word of God addresses it. And one thing is for sure—you can disagree with your friends, but you shouldn't ever disagree with the Bible. If you start to say things like "It's just an outdated book; those verses don't apply anymore," you're treading on very dangerous ground. Why? Well, check out today's verse and you'll see. Jesus Christ is the same—yesterday, today, and forever. That means His Word (the Bible) is the same—yesterday, today, and forever. It's meant to stand the test of time, not change with every new idea that blows in. (And boy, do ideas and trends blow in.)

Stick with what you know to be the truth. Stick with the Bible, and you won't go wrong.

I'll stick with You, Jesus. No way will I allow my opinions to be changed by others. I want to get it right, and I know for a fact that what some of my friends think—even the really smart ones—doesn't always line up with the Bible. Help me stand strong, I pray. Amen.

Day 49

Saying Goodbye

"He will wipe away every tear from their eyes, and death shall be no more, neither shall there be mourning, nor crying, nor pain anymore, for the former things have passed away."

REVELATION 21:4 ESV

Goodbyes are never easy. In fact, they stink.

Sydney learned this firsthand when her grandmother died. She had always been close to the precious woman they all called Nonny. But Sydney had a special place in her heart for her, because Nonny always made her feel loved. They were bonded in many ways, especially over their mutual love of baking. Sydney learned a lot from her grandmother—baking everything from pies to cakes to cookies. What fun they had!

When Nonny was first diagnosed with Alzheimer's, things weren't much different. They still baked together on occasion. But over time, Nonny grew more forgetful. She couldn't remember recipes. Or ingredients. Things in the kitchen got awkward, and Nonny often ended up grumpy and confused.

Then, as the Alzheimer's progressed, she struggled with serious complications and health challenges. Before long, things took a turn, and it was clear Nonny was much worse. The final few weeks of her life were absolutely grueling. The whole family was on edge, knowing it wouldn't be long till she passed from this life.

Sydney was in the room when Nonny breathed her last breath. It was the hardest thing she'd ever witnessed but also the most beautiful, because she knew how much her grandmother loved Jesus and longed for heaven. They had spoken about it many times. The grief was strong, but so was the joy of knowing she would see her grandmother again.

Maybe you've been through a rough patch where you had to say goodbye. Whether you're moving to a new state, changing churches, or saying goodbye to a loved one who is dying, it's tough. Goodbyes are never easy.

Aren't you glad for the promise of heaven? Knowing that one day we'll all be gathered together around God's throne brings such peace. Whatever—or whoever—you're saying goodbye to right now, just remember: Jesus knows the pain of hard goodbyes. He had to leave His mother and His disciples to die on the cross, after all. But He did it, knowing He would one day see them again. You'll see your loved ones too. Heaven awaits, girl!

I'm so grateful for the promise of heaven, Lord! Thank You for my salvation. Amen.

Day 50

Fill Me Up, God!

Hope does not put us to shame, because God's love has been poured into our hearts through the Holy Spirit who has been given to us.

Romans 5:5 esv

Taylor's brother had the craziest appetite ever! Sometimes people would gather around him just to watch him eat. He could down seven or eight pieces of pizza like they were nothing, then top them off with a handful of hot wings. Oh, and lots of soda. Crazy! And was he ever something at an all-you-can-eat buffet. Sometimes Taylor wondered if the restaurant would charge him double because he took advantage of all that food. The boy could seriously put away food!

Maybe you know someone like that. If you've ever heard the old expression "He has a hollow leg," you know what it means: It's too much food to fit in a stomach, so it must be going somewhere else! (Crazy to think about, right?)

Some people don't get full as easily as others. (Maybe you're one of them.) Their appetites are out of control. And it's not just an appetite for food, either. Some people crave experiences. Some crave friendship. Some crave excitement or adventure. Some crave the high that drugs bring or the loss of inhibitions that comes with alcohol. Some crave attention, and they're always seeking to get it in any way they can.

If you know someone who has this kind of appetite, then you know it can be hard to control. Hey, it's like sitting down to Thanksgiving dinner and eating until you feel like you could pop.

Here's the thing, though: God doesn't want us craving the things of this world. He wants you to be filled to the top with Him so that you don't lust after all that the world has to offer.

He's better than Thanksgiving dinner! Time spent with Him will leave you feeling satisfied but not miserable! (No bellyaches!) Best of all, when you've spent time in God's presence, you'll come away with less of a desire for the icky counterfeits this world has to offer.

So what are you waiting for? Dive in, girl! Come to the Lord's table and dine with Him.

I don't want to be full of the things this world has to offer, Jesus. I only want to be filled with Your Spirit, Your truth, and Your peace! I'm going to follow hard after You and nothing else. Fill me up, Lord! Amen.

Day 51

Beauty from Ashes

As for those who grieve over Zion, God has sent me to give them a beautiful crown in exchange for ashes, to anoint them with gladness instead of sorrow, to wrap them in victory, joy, and praise instead of depression and sadness. People will call them magnificent, like great towering trees standing for what is right. They stand to the glory of the Eternal who planted them.

Isaiah 61:3 voice

Imagine you're standing in front of a town that has been burned to the ground. What used to be beautiful buildings are now just barren ruins. An ash heap. You want to cry, looking at it all. What a waste! So much potential gone.

Then, in front of your eyes, the town begins to rebuild. Dust sweeps up into the air and forms beautiful skyscrapers. Roads form. Trees spring to life. Artwork appears. In a matter of minutes, the town is rebuilt better than it was before! Remarkable!

Sound impossible? God does it every day! He brings beauty from ashes. He takes broken, lost, ruined things (and people) and breathes His Spirit into them, causing them to spring to life once more. And guess what? When they come back, they're ten thousand times better than what they were to begin with.

(Hey, it's not that God is showing off. He just can't seem to help Himself! He doesn't do anything small!)

Chelsea watched this happen in her own life. After her parents were killed in a horrible accident, she felt like her life was an ash heap. She went to live with her aunt and cousins. Everything she had known and loved was gone. Chelsea couldn't imagine anything good ever happening again.

But God somehow brought beauty from the ashes of her life. He comforted her, loved her, brought people to show her how much He still cared for her. She went on to live a good life and shared her testimony often, which brought great comfort to others who were going through the grieving process. In other words, He turned her test into a testimony, her tragedy into a triumph. And all because He loved her!

He loves you too. Even if all you see at the moment is ashes. He will—in His own time and in His own way—bring beauty from them. Yes, it seems impossible right now, but remember: God delights in doing the impossible! (You can count on it!)

I've been through some stuff, Jesus. You know, of course, because You were there, loving me through it. Now I need help to move on. Please turn my ashes into something of beauty, I pray. Amen.

Day 52

Not by Might

Then he said to me, "This is the word of the Lord to Zerubbabel: Not by might, nor by power, but by my Spirit, says the Lord of hosts."

Zechariah 4:6 esv

Imagine two men in a weight-lifting competition. One is huge, more than 280 pounds of pure muscle. The other is small, weighing in at 120 pounds. This poor guy has almost no muscle at all. In front of them are barbells. The men are given the following instructions: Keep lifting more and more weight until the strongest of the two wins.

Now picture the competition moving forward. To your surprise, the little guy is doing pretty well. He can lift more than you imagined. And you're shocked to see that he easily takes down the big guy in the end. Wow! Never saw that coming, did you?

Sound improbable? You might read this and think, *Yeah. . .no. Doesn't happen like that.* But, here's a fun truth straight from the Word of God. Spiritual muscles outweigh physical ones. Don't believe it? Ask David, who took down the mighty giant Goliath. Ask Joshua, who marched around the walls of Jericho. Ask Hannah, who prayed for a child and eventually had baby Samuel. Ask anyone who has ever witnessed a miracle in their life in spite of obstacles.

The little guy (you!) really can win when God is on your side. And remember, it's not by might. It's not by power. It's by His Spirit.

Read that again. *It's not by might.* (No matter how hard you work out, there are some battles you'll never win without God's help.) It's not by power. (You can have superhuman strength but still fail without His Spirit leading the way.) It's only by the supernatural Spirit of God that you can make it through the challenges you'll face, girl. (When you think of it like that, you have to realize that it's about God, not you!)

Here's an amazing truth: The Holy Spirit lives inside of you from the moment you accept Jesus Christ as Savior and Lord of your life. (You have done that, right?) His Spirit gives power, brings comfort, whispers words of encouragement, and gives you energy to get through your day. (Tip: You'll never make it without the daily infilling of the Holy Spirit, so ask for more and more of Him!)

I need more of Your Spirit, Lord! That's where my power comes from. I can try all day long on my own, but I will fail. Fill me today, I pray. Make me a spiritual powerhouse! Amen.

Day 53

Desensitization

I appeal to you therefore, brothers, by the mercies of God, to present your bodies as a living sacrifice, holy and acceptable to God, which is your spiritual worship. Do not be conformed to this world, but be transformed by the renewal of your mind, that by testing you may discern what is the will of God, what is good and acceptable and perfect.

ROMANS 12:1–2 ESV

Maybe you've heard the old story about how you can put a frog in a pot of water and slowly bring it to a boil. He won't even realize he's facing certain death at first. He won't try to escape, because the water is comfortable. Then it gets warmer until it's borderline hot. And the hotter the water gets, the more unable he is to escape. After a while, he simply gives up. The battle is over. He got duped!

You might not understand the frog analogy until you take a look around you at the way society is trying to desensitize you.

Music, for example. Though you might say, "Oh, it's just music," the truth is, the lyrics and motivation behind the songs are often as far away from godly as you can imagine. In fact, some of the lyrics truly break God's heart (and should break yours). But you find yourself singing along. Why? Because you've heard the song so many times it becomes a part of you. (Dangerous, if you really think about it.)

The same is true with movies. Violence. Sex. Inappropriate behaviors. It's all in the shows and movies you watch. But you're so desensitized that you hardly notice it anymore. Who cares if a movie is loaded with bad words? You hear them every day, right?

Here's the point: God's heart is still broken over these things. And He longs for you to remain so pure that your heart is broken too. It's not going to be easy to remain sensitive to these things. It's going to take awareness on your part as well as nudges from His Spirit. But if your eyes are wide open, if you want to make your Father's heart happy, you'll see just what the enemy is up to, and you'll run as fast as you can in the opposite direction.

Thank You, Jesus, for opening my eyes to the things of this world that I should avoid. Make me sensitive. I don't want to break Your heart. Instead, I want to be more like You. Thank You for leading me, Holy Spirit! Amen.

Day 54

Beautiful Mistakes

Indeed, we all make many mistakes. For if we could control our tongues, we would be perfect and could also control ourselves in every other way.

James 3:2 NLT

Autumn made a mistake in judgment. While driving the car alone for the very first time, she thought she had enough time to make a quick left turn before the oncoming vehicle got there.

Wrong.

She turned. . .and got smashed! Her mom's SUV took a hard hit to the front passenger side. And the lady who hit her wasn't exactly happy that Autumn caused this accident. Turned out, her car—an expensive sports car—was brand spanking new. Just off the showroom floor, in fact. Ouch!

Autumn felt terrible for what happened. She just couldn't get over it. Even though insurance covered the cost, it raised her parents' rates with their provider. And it seemed like every day she got more bad news. Her mom's car was totaled, which meant the family had to start from scratch, looking for a new vehicle. And the woman with the sports car? She was cranky through the whole process. Even the insurance adjuster was rude. Why did all of this have to happen? Oh yes, because

Autumn made a teensy-tiny mistake in judgment, one that turned out to be huge!

Maybe you've made some mistakes in judgment too. Maybe you caused an accident or some sort of grief for someone else, and you feel horrible about it. What started small has morphed into something gigantic. And you want to crawl into a hole!

Oh, sweet girl, we all make mistakes. Anyone who says they don't? Well, they're just not being honest. The key is to learn from them. They can only be beautiful if you allow yourself to learn the lessons and move forward.

Autumn's mom ended up with a new SUV that had all kinds of bells and whistles (the cool stuff). The lady in the sports car? Her vehicle was fixed in no time. And Autumn? She was a lot more careful when making left-hand turns.

In other words, it all worked out in the end.

Just like it always does.

I trust You to turn my mistakes into something of beauty, Jesus. Even at the lowest point, I know You can still turn things around. Help me to be extra careful, but when things go wrong, teach me how to extend grace to myself, I pray! Amen.

Day 55

Abba, Daddy

This resurrection life you received from God is not a timid, grave-tending life. It's adventurously expectant, greeting God with a childlike "What's next, Papa?" God's Spirit touches our spirits and confirms who we really are. We know who he is, and we know who we are: Father and children. And we know we are going to get what's coming to us—an unbelievable inheritance! We go through exactly what Christ goes through. If we go through the hard times with him, then we're certainly going to go through the good times with him!

ROMANS 8:15–17 MSG

Mandy had father issues. She never really knew her own dad. He took off before she was born. And her mom had a few relationships with guys over the years that were—to put it bluntly—rough. Really rough. Let's just say Mama wasn't that great at picking out guys.

So, yeah, Mandy never really had a good dad as an example to know what one would look like.

Her best friend, Trina, though? Her dad was amazing. He was like that father from a classic 1960s TV show—always showing up at every ball game, every choir concert, every ballet recital. He brought flowers, gave hugs, and showered Trina with compliments.

Mandy wondered what that would feel like.

Maybe you're wondering too. Maybe you don't have a godly father. You've never known the kind of love Trina experienced. But that doesn't mean it has to stay that way.

Take a look at today's verse. God wants you to know that He's your Daddy. It's true! He's been there for every big (and small!) event in your life. He showed up when no one else did. When you were crying in the night? He was right there. When you made an A on that biology test? He saw that and celebrated. When you felt like quitting, He was right there, whispering in your ear, "Don't give up, kiddo!" And because His fatherly voice gave you courage, you kept going.

The Hebrew word the Bible uses to describe God is *Abba*. Translated, it means "Daddy." God wants to have a close, daddy relationship with you. So even if you don't have an earthly father you can draw close to, you definitely have the perfect Daddy God, who longs to wrap you in His arms today.

I trust in You, my Daddy God! Thank You for loving me with an everlasting love. I'm so grateful to You, my heavenly Father! Amen.

Day 56

You're a Real Sport!

An athlete is not crowned unless he competes according to the rules.

2 TIMOTHY 2:5 ESV

Jesus never really talked about sports, at least not the ones we enjoy today. It's not like He said, "Hey guys, I want you to root for My favorite team!" Nope. There's really nothing in the Bible like that. So what can you learn from the Word of God about that sport you love so much?

First, don't give up. Like today's verse says, you can persevere. Even if you're not the best server on the volleyball team. Even if you can't get the ball over the net every time. You can still keep trying.

Next, you can learn a lot about sportsmanship, because we see lots of verses like Proverbs 27:17 (ESV): "Iron sharpens iron, and one man sharpens another." God wants you to get along and work together, to be a team player. (It's "we," not "me"!) As your coach likes to say, "There's no *I* in *team*!" And she's right! It's about the group, not the individual. (Sounds a lot like the church, right? It's about all of us working together to spread the gospel to the world.)

Finally, you can learn about using your gifts and abilities.

The Bible says that you were given specific gifts. Maybe, in your case, you have a special ability to pitch. So in you go as a pitcher on the girls' softball team. Or maybe you've proven that your gift is leadership, so your gymnastics coach chooses you to be the captain of your team. Your gifts and abilities can develop and grow over a period of months or years. Before you know it, you'll be even better!

One more thing you might want to keep in mind: You never see a basketball team stop at halftime and say, "You know what, guys? Let's just call it a day." Nope. They get right back in the game, even if they're falling behind and not getting the points they hoped. They set their sights on what's in front of them, not what they've left behind. And many, many times they'll turn things around and win the game. That's a great lesson for you too! Don't give up, girl!

No matter which sport you enjoy, learn from it. Let your coach, your fellow players, and your own talents draw you closer to Jesus every step of the way.

I'm so glad You added me to Your team lineup, Jesus! Thanks for teaching me all I need to know about being a good sport. Amen.

Day 57

Shine Your Light

"In the same way, let your light shine before others, so that they may see your good works and give glory to your Father who is in heaven."

MATTHEW 5:16 ESV

Maybe when you were a kid you used to sing that sweet children's song that says, "This little light of mine, I'm gonna let it shine." Shining your light sounded so easy back then. But living out your faith as a teen in the twenty-first century? Well, that has turned out to be a little harder than you thought it would be, hasn't it? These days people make it difficult to share the gospel message. They're not open to hearing about God's way of doing things, because most of them are so busy living however they want.

So let's think of some ways you can shine your light even when darkness threatens to consume those around you. First, the finest light you can ever shine is the love of Jesus. Some would say, "Yes, love those who are different from you. They need your love." And they do. But, girl, sometimes the hardest people to show loving affection to are the ones you live with. Those siblings. Those parents. That BFF who grates on your nerves. These people need your love too, so shine your light, even inside the walls of your own house.

Another way you shine your light is by demonstrating the opposite spirit. What does this mean? When you would ordinarily respond with anger, you choose kindness instead. When most people would make a big deal out of something, you decide to make a small deal out of it. Whatever the temptation might be, do the opposite thing. You'll leave people guessing what you're going to do next!

Another way to shine God's light is to share your testimony. The word *testimony* is just a fancy way of saying "your story." How did you come to know Jesus? When did you give your heart to Him? What did He save you from? These are all part of your testimony.

Shining your light doesn't mean you have to stand on a street corner and shout, "Repent, sinner!" It's really just as simple as living your life authentically in front of a watching world.

I'll go on shining my light, Jesus.
This world is pretty dark right now,
but I'll do my best to light things up! Amen.

Day 58

Self-Control

Like a city broken into and left without a wall,
so is a person who lacks self-control.

Proverbs 25:28 GW

Whitney *loved* chocolate. Loved, loved, loved it. And once she got started, watch out! She couldn't seem to stop. The girl had no self-control. The same was true whenever she sat down to eat a bowl of ice cream. One scoop wasn't enough. Oh no. Two? Nah. The girl wanted a full bowl of the creamy, yummy stuff and wouldn't stop until her belly was full.

Maybe you can relate. You struggle with self-control too. Whether it's sweets, soda, or the number of hours you devote to your cell phone, you're hooked.

So what's a girl to do? How do you break the cycle and begin to exhibit self-control? The answer is found in today's verse: A person who lacks self-control is like a city left without a wall.

Okay, okay, so you're wondering what that means exactly. Good point. Back in the old days, cities were "fortified," meaning they all had giant walls around them. The walls kept their enemies from coming in and destroying them.

But here's the thing: Your enemy (Satan) is a lot like those enemies back then. He wants to come in and “take your city.” Everything God has built in your life is up for grabs when you leave yourself unarmed, and Satan knows it. In fact, he’s counting on it! He wants you to let down your guard.

Giving up your self-control opens you up to the enemy’s schemes. It’s that simple, really.

Need an example? Say you wanted to hang out with your friends, but you knew they were about to do something your parents wouldn’t agree with. You decided to go for it and not let your mom and dad know the whole story. That lack of self-control brings the walls down and allows the enemy to get his foot in the door. And once he’s in—well, you know the rest. He won’t stop until he has done as much damage as possible.

You can rebuild the walls of your city today by exercising self-control—in your relationships, your speech, and your actions. Then your city will be fortified. There’s not a chance that sly enemy will sneak through!

Thanks for teaching me how to protect my city, Jesus. I won’t let down my guard. I will exhibit self-control. Amen.

Day 59

Waiting: Not Easy but Worth It!

Those who trust in the Lord will find new strength. They will soar high on wings like eagles. They will run and not grow weary. They will walk and not faint.

Isaiah 40:31 NLT

No one likes to wait. Give people the choice between "Get it now!" and "Wait ten years and then you can have it!" and which one do you think they'll choose? They'll want it now, of course!

Why do you suppose people feel that way? We live in an instantaneous world, that's why! We sign onto the internet in seconds, get our food from the microwave or fast-food restaurants, and stream online services for our favorite TV show, which we can watch whenever we like, at any time of day. (Hey, back in the olden days people had to wait days or even weeks for their favorite shows to come on; and if they happened to forget, too bad! There was no way to record them. No kidding!)

These days everything happens at lightning speed. So when it doesn't—when things take longer—we lose patience.

Here's the thing about waiting, though. When you wait,

God renews your strength. To renew something means it's "made new." And isn't that what you want, for your strength to be made new every day? You don't have to wake up feeling drained with no energy. You can bounce out of bed (no, really!) and dive into your day, excited and refreshed for the tasks ahead.

So don't grumble about waiting, girl. Everything happens in God's time, anyway. Keep putting one foot in front of the other. Keep trusting, even when you can't see results. You're mounting up with wings like eagles even now. So, when the right moment comes, you'll take off flying! You'll soar because you've been building the spiritual and emotional muscles to face the tasks ahead. You'll be so strong!

And remember, the people around you are still waiting on God too. Sure, some of them are in great seasons. They're getting the things they prayed for. But others? They're just where you are, wondering if or when God is going to come through for them.

He will. He always does. It might not look like you envision, but He always fulfills His promises. He never lets you down.

So. . .wait. And while you're waiting, go ahead and praise God for what's coming!

Lord, I get it! I'll persevere. I'll wait with patience and joy. I know that waiting is making me stronger, and I want to soar when the time comes. So I'll praise You, even while I'm waiting. Amen.

Day 60

Who You Say I Am

Beloved, we are God's children now, and what we will be has not yet appeared; but we know that when he appears we shall be like him, because we shall see him as he is.

1 JOHN 3:2 ESV

She hurt your feelings. Again. She made some biting remarks, and they stung. Tears came to your eyes right away, but you did your best to brush them away. How long will you go on letting her get to you? Forever?

No doubt there are people in your world who have a knack for putting you down. They get their digs in, and it hurts. Some might call you ugly. Or fat. Or lazy. Or unpopular. Some might say, "You're so stupid" or "Why can't you get your act together like your sister?" These words cause pain. They're like a knife in your heart.

And sometimes—just keeping it real—we speak these things over ourselves. When we do poorly on a test, we convince ourselves that we're not smart. When we fail at a task, we think we'll never get it. When we look in the mirror, we see plain or ugly staring back at us. Our internal thoughts are as hateful as the ugly words that mean people speak over us.

But God? He doesn't say any of those things. When He looks

at you, He says things like these: “I forgive you for the things you mess up” (1 John 1:9). “You are created in My image!” (Genesis 1:27). “You are beautiful to Me” (Song of Solomon 4:7). “You are worthy of love” (Romans 5:8). “I loved you so much, in fact, that I gave My life for you!” (John 3:16).

Oh, but it goes on! He says, “You can do all things through Me!” (Philippians 4:13). “No weapon formed against you will prosper!” (Isaiah 54:17). “You are protected” (2 Thessalonians 3:3). “You can have peace, even in troubled times” (John 16:33). “You are a daughter of the Most High King” (1 John 3:1).

When you stop to think about all of the times—and ways—God says who you are, it’s easy to forget about the ugly things people say. So who will you listen to today, God or man?

I’ll listen to You, Jesus! You’re the one who speaks life over me! You’re the one who speaks hope. Your words are better. Thanks for speaking over me, Your beloved child. Amen.

Day 61

Playing by the Rules

I long for your guiding principles.
Give me a new life in your righteousness.

Psalm 119:40 GW

Kiera made her own rules. If the group leader said, "Be here by seven," she'd come rolling in around 7:20 every time. If her parents said, "Watch your sister," she would pawn the task off on someone else. And if her teacher said, "That assignment has to include a bibliography," she would argue when she got her paper back that bibliographies were dumb and unnecessary.

Basically, she would just do what she wanted. And much of the time she got away with it. People stopped arguing with her because she made things so miserable when she didn't get her way.

Here's the problem with that. A day will come when girls like Kiera have a boss who won't put up with her attitude. Or a mortgage company that sends a foreclosure notice when she doesn't follow through with the payments they agreed on. Or kids who are disappointed because Mom is always making promises but not delivering on them.

You get the idea. The time will come when that sort of lifestyle will backfire, and there will be a price to pay that might be pretty steep.

Rules are made for a reason. They're not meant to hurt you but to guide you. Remember when you were young and you went bowling? Your parents pushed the button to bring down the side rails so that the ball wouldn't go in the gutter. That's what happens when you follow the rules. They'll keep your proverbial ball from rolling into the gutter. (And let's face it, it's no fun to roll a bunch of gutter balls! You'll lose the game.)

Instead of fighting the rules, pray about them. Ask God's opinion. See what His Word says. Then ask for the courage to do the right thing. It won't be easy, especially if you're used to getting your own way (or playing by your own rules); but if you can turn this part of your life around while you're still young, you'll have a much smoother adulthood. And remember, you're in training right now. It's better to get it right when you're young and save yourself heartache when you're older!

I'll learn my lessons, Jesus. You've given me biblical guidelines for a reason. No gutter balls for me! I'll play by Your rules, not my own, but I will definitely need Your help with that. Amen.

Day 62

In the Middle of the Storm

A violent windstorm came up. The waves were breaking into the boat so that it was quickly filling up. But [Jesus] was sleeping on a cushion in the back of the boat. So they woke him up and said to him, "Teacher, don't you care that we're going to die?" Then he got up, ordered the wind to stop, and said to the sea, "Be still, absolutely still!" The wind stopped blowing, and the sea became very calm.

MARK 4:37–39 GW

The disciples spent a lot of time in a boat. Some of them were fishermen, after all. So they were in their comfort zone on the water.

But not in the middle of a massive storm. And that's exactly what happened one time. Jesus, exhausted after a day of teaching and healing, was snoozing in the back of the boat while a storm raged overhead. The disciples decided to wake Him up with the words "Don't You care if we drown?"

Let's stop right there. Have you ever been sound asleep during a rainstorm? You didn't hear the thunder. You didn't see the lightning. You were snoozing away, enjoying your rest. Then your kid sister climbed into bed with you, crying.

She woke you up, and before long you were panicked too.

Good thing Jesus didn't panic. Instead, He spoke to the storm, and it calmed down at once. Then He turned to the guys and asked them a very important question: "Why are you afraid? Do you still have no faith?" (v. 40 NCV).

Ouch.

No doubt they felt bad for waking Him up but were still very relieved that the storm had stopped.

That's kind of how it is with us too. We get panicked when life's storms blow in. Someone gets really sick. Someone loses a job. Someone stops talking to us. Someone starts a rumor that's not true. We're pretty sure we won't make it through, so we call on Jesus. And He calms things down every time.

Here's a little-known fact: When you walk with Jesus on a daily basis, when you have His Spirit living inside of you, you don't have to panic—at all. You can be the one snoozing, completely peaceful. In other words, life's chaos doesn't have to knock you for a loop every single time. The Spirit of God can infuse you with supernatural peace to ride above the waves!

I get it, Jesus. I can have peace in the storm just like You did. Help me not to overreact when hard times come. Calm my heart, I pray. Give me peace. Amen.

Day 63

When Hope's Dream Drags On

When hope's dream seems to drag on and on, the delay can be depressing. But when at last your dream comes true, life's sweetness will satisfy your soul.

PROVERBS 13:12 TPT

Sometimes things just take awhile. You can hope for something, but it might not come to pass exactly when (or how) you think it will. And let's be honest: When you start feeling those familiar pangs of disappointment, when those "It's never going to happen" feelings creep over you, life can get depressing. There's nothing worse than reaching the point where you just simply give up.

Megan reached that point. She was absolutely sure she would make first chair in the choir. Of all the first sopranos, there were only two or three others who could hit the high notes the way she could. So she worked harder than ever. Megan kept hoping. And praying. And wishing. And practicing. And telling everyone that one day it would happen. She never doubted it for a second.

Only, it never seemed to happen. And before long she almost lost hope. Her heart just wasn't in it anymore. When she reached the point of giving up, depression set in. What was the sense of working hard—on anything? If it hadn't worked out last time, it probably wouldn't next time either. Why try anything?

See how the enemy works? He plants seeds of doubt in your mind, and before long you're spreading them all around. Everything becomes exaggerated in your mind.

In the end, Megan decided to keep going. Good thing she did! She made first chair her senior year. And good things will happen for you too!

Okay, so maybe it didn't work out last time. You're disappointed. But that doesn't mean your next dream is doomed to failure. It could happen, girl—but only if you don't give up.

Go ahead and hope. Go ahead and dream. But remember, it's God's plans that come to pass in the end, not your own. And believe this: What God has planned for you is a billion times better than anything you could dream up for yourself.

I don't want to be a quitter, Jesus. Even if I'm facing disappointments, help me not to give up. I want to stick with it and see how far I can go. I'm going to need Your help, for sure! Amen.

Day 64

When You're Disappointed

This hope will not lead to disappointment. For we know how dearly God loves us, because he has given us the Holy Spirit to fill our hearts with his love.

Romans 5:5 NLT

Sienna could hardly wait for Christmas. She had asked her parents for the perfect gift, a new laptop, one with all of the latest, greatest features. Sure, her mom's work hours had just been cut. And yes, it was going to be a "slim" Christmas, as her dad liked to call it. But she figured they would still come through for her. She really needed it, after all, and her parents realized that.

But Christmas came and there was no laptop under the tree. Instead, she got something completely unexpected—decor for her bedroom. Pink pillow shams and curtains.

And she wasn't happy. Oh, sure, she did her best to look happy, but really—stuff for her room? They called that a present?

Inside, Sienna was very disappointed. Let down. She felt completely bummed that she didn't get what she had been waiting for.

If you've ever been disappointed, you know that feeling well. Maybe your family had plans to go to a big theme park and your plans got canceled. Or maybe you set your sights on trying out for the lead in the school play, only to find out the date of the play conflicted with a prior obligation at church.

Disappointments can be painful, for sure. And they never seem fair.

Here's a great truth to make you feel better: God will never disappoint you. Take a look at today's verse. Hope in Him never leads to disappointment. Why? Because it reminds us how dearly we are loved by Him. And when you're truly loved (as Sienna was by her parents), love trumps stuff. Love is better. Love is greater. Love is more important. And the Holy Spirit pours love out like a fountain, filling your heart.

Hey, it's kind of hard to be mad at someone who loves you like that. So, if your parents have disappointed you somehow, just remember how much they adore you. And remember, you've probably disappointed others in the past too. And they still know you love them.

Don't let disappointment rule the day. Step away from it, girl!

You'll never disappoint me, Jesus. I know You love me, and I trust that You're always thinking of what's best for me. Help me not to be disappointed when things don't go my way, I pray. Amen.

Day 65

Never Worry about Anything

Never worry about anything. But in every situation let God know what you need in prayers and requests while giving thanks. Then God's peace, which goes beyond anything we can imagine, will guard your thoughts and emotions through Christ Jesus.

PHILIPPIANS 4:6–7 GW

Courtney struggled with anxiety. It kept her knotted up on the inside. She just couldn't seem to help herself. Schoolwork made her anxious. Being around people made her nervous. Trying to make friends? Yeah, that made her anxious too. She would break out in a cold sweat whenever she had to talk to strangers. So she didn't do it very often.

Some people would just say she was the nervous sort, and that was a possibility. But here's the thing—anxiety is controllable. Sure, it's not easy to say no to anxiety, but you have to try. Why? Because Jesus said so! In fact, He made it pretty clear in today's verse just how He feels about it: "Never worry about anything."

Whoa. That's a tall order.

Anything? Like *anything* anything? Even sicknesses like

cancer? Financial problems? Failing grades? I'm not supposed to be anxious about that stuff?

"In every situation let God know what you need."

Okay, that helps. The big stuff doesn't seem quite as overwhelming when I know I can bring it to God.

". . .while giving thanks."

I can give thanks while going through something awful? Is that a thing? Really, Jesus?

"Then God's peace, which goes beyond anything we can imagine, will guard your thoughts. . ."

Well now, that's cool! When I'm going through the worst of the worst, God's right there to bring peace and to help calm down those crazy thoughts going through my brain. If I can get my thoughts under control, I'm not as anxious.

". . .and emotions through Christ Jesus."

Jesus cares about my emotions too? Those tears? That pain in my heart?

He does care, you know. He's not minimizing the hard things you've been through. Not at all. But He wants You to know that He's right there, ready to help you deal with those anxieties and to remind you that you are never alone. So give them to Him today, and watch as His peace sweeps over you and calms things down.

Thank You for helping me get beyond this anxiety, Lord! It's exciting to know that You've given me a way out of worry. Help me, I pray. Amen.

Day 66

The Good and the Bad

"Catch the foxes for us, the little foxes that spoil the vineyards, for our vineyards are in blossom."

Song of Solomon 2:15 ESV

The good and the bad live alongside each other. Every day good things happen. You wake up. You have food to eat. You enjoy breath in your lungs. You live with a family that loves you. But at the same time, bad things happen. People you love get sick. Others are abused. Friends end up fighting. Teachers get mad at you.

It's so confusing. Why can't everything be good all at the same time? How come great days have to be ruined with bad stuff that you never expected? How come your sister has to be in a terrible mood on the one day when everything is going great? Why did your science teacher have to pick that one perfect day to throw a pop quiz?

Whenever something comes up that threatens to spoil the good, it's like a "little fox." What's a little fox, you ask? Take a look at today's verse from Song of Solomon. In this story, the vineyards are in full bloom. (Interpretation: Things are going great!) Then, along come the little foxes. They "spoil" the vine. In other words, those baby foxes get in there and mess things up. They wreck the vineyard. (Think about the damage a three-year-old could do to your bedroom.) A little bit of trouble does a great amount of damage.

That's how it is in your life too. Sometimes you let the little foxes spoil your day. You get so hyper-focused on the one bad thing that happened that you forget to see all of the good things that happened too.

Little foxes will inevitably come. You do what you can to protect your vineyard (your heart); but the enemy is always on the prowl, trying to knock you off your game. And he has some skills, that's for sure. But you can't let those little foxes ruin all of the good. It's still good, even when bad things crop up.

One way to focus more on the good is to thank God for the little things—the air in your lungs, the home you live in, the food in your belly. When you remember to praise Him for the good, then the bad doesn't seem so bad!

Thank You for the good things, Lord! I don't ever want to forget that my vineyard is thriving! My heart is on fire for You. I won't let those pesky little foxes spoil everything. I'll guard my heart and keep it safe. Amen.

Day 67

Fix Your Mind, Girl!

"You keep him in perfect peace whose mind is stayed on you, because he trusts in you. Trust in the Lord forever, for the Lord God is an everlasting rock."

Isaiah 26:3–4 ESV

You're super stressed out today, and you hate the way it feels. You know you should give your problems to Jesus, but it's so hard. To do so would mean you have to let go, and that's not easy. Holding tightly to them? It's hard to unwind your fingers, right? God's going to have to wrestle your problems out of your hands. He would much prefer that you open those hands and give Him your problems, by the way.

Sure, it's not easy. But here's the deal, girl: You need to pray for the faith to let go. This problem is bigger than you. It just is. And things are never going to get better as long as you insist on doing everything yourself. (Hello. Some things are just too big for humans to handle!) What you need right now is faith the size of a teeny-tiny mustard seed. Jesus said that mustard-seed-sized faith is enough to perform miracles, and isn't that what you need? A miracle?

Jesus told His followers, "If you have faith as a mustard seed, you will say to this mountain, 'Move from here to over there,' and it would move over. You will be able to do anything" (Matthew 17:20 NLV).

See? It doesn't take much faith to turn things around. So do your part, and God will do His. Pray. Then do your best to let go. Don't sit around staring at your problems. The longer you stare at them, the bigger they'll get. (You've probably already figured this out.) Instead, fix your eyes on Jesus. And while you're at it, go ahead and confess to Him that you've left Him out of the equation for too long. The drama held you spellbound, and you couldn't seem to remember that He had all of the answers—not you.

Fix your mind on Him. He's the only one who can give answers and peace.

I'm sorry for the times I left You out, Jesus! I want to keep my mind on You, not the swirling, terrible problems I'm facing. I know You'll show me what to do, Jesus! Give me mustard-seed faith so that I can move mountains, I pray. Amen.

Day 68

Bring Him the Awkward Stuff

The Holy Spirit helps us in our weakness. For example, we don't know what God wants us to pray for. But the Holy Spirit prays for us with groanings that cannot be expressed in words.

ROMANS 8:26 NLT

Being a girl is tough. All that monthly stuff? It can be a real pain. Cramps. Pain. Bloating. Feeling weird? Yeah, you're not a fan, but what can you do?

And even when you're not dealing with all that, other things about being female can get on your nerves too! Putting up with the other girls, for instance. They can be difficult to deal with sometimes. Factor in siblings who don't get along, cute boys who don't seem to notice you exist, and life can get pretty complicated.

It's not always easy to know who you can talk to about the awkward stuff. But God is right there, arms outstretched, saying, "You know you can bring that to Me today, right? You can!"

The really cool thing about God? Nothing is awkward with Him. *Nothing*. Think of the most embarrassing thing you might have to say to a friend or loved one, and then imagine saying it to God. He won't be shocked at all. In fact, He will be really, really glad you trusted Him with that information.

Jasmine found this out personally. When she started her period at the age of twelve, she didn't like the way she felt. Grumpy. Moody. And talk about painful cramps! Why didn't anyone warn her? She wanted to talk to someone about it, but Mom just got embarrassed whenever the subject came up. Her older sister? Yeah, she was always too busy. And her kid sister? Well, she was too young.

Jasmine found a good friend who was going through the same thing, so she confided in her. But in the middle of the night when tears unexpectedly flowed, she decided she'd better talk to Jesus about the situation too. Would He understand?

She poured out her heart and told Him all of the things that were worrying her. Then, miraculously, she fell sound asleep, completely peaceful.

No matter what you're facing, girl, Jesus is still right there. And yeah, He gets it. Even the girl stuff. So never be afraid to come to Him.

Father, do You have a little while to
chat about something kind of awkward?
This is totally weird, but I really need to talk
to You about ____________________. Amen.

Day 69

Talk to Jesus

"Then you will call to me. You will come and pray to me, and I will answer you."

Jeremiah 29:12 GNT

Tiffany was a talker. She could talk your ear off. In fact, people would often ask her to stop talking, but she found silence difficult. So on and on she would go—sharing all of the details of her day, the good, the bad, and the ugly. She wouldn't leave out a thing. Every hurt, every joy, every low point, every high—she spilled the tea on all of it. She also talked about the people she liked and the ones she wasn't so crazy about. She talked about the ups and downs with her friends, her enemies, and the random people who drove her crazy. She would tell you anything and everything—from the mundane to the spectacular—and all with great zeal.

Weirdly, though, she hardly ever talked to Jesus about any of that stuff. Oh, she was a Christian. No doubt about that. She went to church on Sundays. Sometimes on Wednesdays too. And she did all the churchy things. But when it came to her prayer life, she wasn't really a talker—to God.

It took awhile to figure it out, but Tiffany finally realized that instead of praying, she'd been telling all of her troubles to her friends. And her siblings. And her parents. Instead of sharing all of her joys with Jesus, she shared them with her loved ones.

Here's the point: It's good to share things with your family and friends, but don't leave God out! He created you to be in fellowship with Him. Picture Him standing at the door of your heart every single day, just waiting for you to answer.

Open the door, girl. Let Him in. Talk to Him. Tell Him all of those same things you're sharing with others. Then tell Him the things you're not willing to tell anyone—those deep, dark secrets. The things you're struggling with when no one is around.

Talk to Jesus. Don't make Him wait any longer.

I'm sorry I haven't been talking to You as much, Jesus. I don't do it on purpose! Sometimes I get so busy that I forget. Other times I spill the tea to my friends and family and get all talked out. I don't want You to have to wait at my heart's door any longer! Come on in! Let's chat! Amen.

Day 70

Control Freak

Many are the plans in the mind of a man,
but it is the purpose of the Lord that will stand.

Proverbs 19:21 ESV

Julia was a bit of a control freak. She wanted things a certain way. Her room? It had to be perfect. Her grades? Straight As. She didn't want anyone touching her stuff. It was hers, after all. And when it came to group projects? She had to be the one in charge. Everyone knew better than to try to take the lead when they were paired with her. She was going to be the boss, and that's just the way things were.

Maybe you know a few control freaks. Maybe you are one. Once you've had a taste of being the boss, it's kind of hard to go back, right?

Here's the thing, though: *Always* having to be the boss is not a good thing for you or for those you're bossing around. Sure, maybe God gave you some natural leadership abilities, but humble yourself, girl! Give others a chance. You don't always have to be the one calling the shots or making the decisions. How will others grow if you're always taking charge? They'll never have a chance, and you'll get burned out!

Want to know a sad truth? Control freaks really freak

out when life gets uncontrollable—like when a parent gets cancer or a hurricane blows in. (Hey, when you're used to getting your way or making things happen, it's quite a shock to find out you're not really as "in charge" as you thought.) It's better to release control now, during a calm season, than to face a rough season still trying to fix everything. (Tip: It won't work—you can't fix the rough seasons!)

Don't worry! God will show you how to let go so that He's free to move on your behalf. He longs for you to put your trust in Him, after all; and that's only truly possible if you give Him the reins. So what are you waiting for? Open those tightly clenched fists and let it go, girl. Let it go.

I've been a control freak, Jesus! I'll admit it.
I like to call the shots, to tell others what to do.
But You're showing me that it's not good to
think that I'm the boss of the world. The only
one who truly reigns is You, Lord, so I open my
hands and give the control back to You. Amen.

Day 71

Flexibility

I appeal to you therefore, brothers, by the mercies of God, to present your bodies as a living sacrifice, holy and acceptable to God, which is your spiritual worship. Do not be conformed to this world, but be transformed by the renewal of your mind, that by testing you may discern what is the will of God, what is good and acceptable and perfect.

ROMANS 12:1–2 ESV

Trinity's years as a gymnast really paid off. All of that time on the balance beam, uneven bars, and vault really developed her abilities. And talk about some skills on the floor. Wow, that girl could flip with the best of them!

Even though she didn't make it to nationals like she hoped, Trinity had a potential career ahead of her as a coach. And best of all, the years in the gym had really stretched her tendons and ligaments and made her extremely flexible. She could do the splits like crazy! And backbends were no big deal to her. People were always amazed at her flexibility.

You might not be bendable like Trinity, but God still wants to stretch you! It's one thing to be physically flexible, and another to be flexible when life throws you curveballs. Like when you think one thing's going to happen but then the opposite happens. You're expecting a family vacation but get a pandemic. You're hoping for an A on the exam but end up bombing it. You're counting on money to come in, and it doesn't.

What then? When you're given lemons instead of lemonade, what do you do?

The same thing Trinity did. You exhibit flexibility. Instead of freaking out—and let's face it, anyone can do that—you remain calm, cool, and collected. You lead by example. Others will see that you're not in a panic, and they will learn to react the same way.

When you stay calm, you bring honor to God because you are showing that you have trust in Him. And remember, the more flexible you are this time, the more flexible you'll be the next because your spiritual tendons and ligaments are being s-t-r-e-t-c-h-e-d. They're getting a workout, and that's a good thing. Before long, you'll be bending over backward with ease! Spiritually speaking, of course.

Lord, I want to be more flexible. I don't want to be stubborn or set in my ways. Get me ready for the curveballs so that I can stay calm when they come my way. Stretch me, I pray. Amen.

Day 72

Well, That Was Awkward

Obviously, I'm not trying to win the approval of people, but of God. If pleasing people were my goal, I would not be Christ's servant.

Galatians 1:10 NLT

"I made a total goober out of myself."

Ever spoken those words? Maybe you embarrassed yourself royally in front of your friends. Or worse, strangers. There's nothing like saying or doing the wrong thing to bring the worst kind of attention to yourself. Like that time you passed gas while walking down the hallway at school. (Ahem.) Or that time you glanced in the bathroom mirror and realized you had something in your nose—right after having a great conversation with a cute guy. Or that infamous time you messed up a major presentation in front of your whole class. You felt like running from the room. Could you just pretend it didn't happen? Pretty please?

Alexandra knew what that felt like. There she was, in the middle of telling a story, when something slipped out about her mom that was supposed to be private. She embarrassed her mother, who was left feeling confused and upset. And all because she was trying to show off with a funny story. Oh, Alexandra didn't mean to cause a problem. It just happened. But she couldn't take it back. (Hey, you can't untell a story, now, can you?)

Maybe things have "just happened" with you too. You got caught in the middle of an awkward situation and couldn't seem to turn things around. Some things just feel impossible to fix.

Here's some good news: No matter what you've messed up, God can fix it. (Tip: This isn't an invitation to mess something up on purpose.) He's really good at getting you past the awkward moments and back to normal. You may face natural consequences. For sure, if you've hurt someone's feelings, you're going to have to make things right. But you can do it, girl!

Here's a key word you can count on to help: *grace*. When you mess up, give yourself grace. Don't beat yourself up. You will get past this awkward feeling. No, really. It might take a while, but the embarrassing moments will soon be nothing but a memory.

Jesus, I messed up, and now I feel like such a goober! Help me move on, please! I don't like the way this feels. Thanks for forgiving me for my mistakes and giving me another chance! Amen.

Day 73

It's Just Too Hard

Be happy in your hope. Do not give up when trouble comes. Do not let anything stop you from praying.

Romans 12:12 NLV

"No way. No how. I'm not gonna do it. Not today, maybe not ever."

Have you ever spoken those words? There are days when you just can't. Or at least you *feel* like you can't. So you don't. You just freeze in place and do nothing.

Here's the funny thing about feelings, though—they don't always tell the truth. Sometimes they lie to you. In fact, they're big fat liars much of the time! And here's something else you need to know: If you only choose to do what you *feel* like you can do, then you won't do much.

Annabella felt like that. After going through a rough day on Monday, she woke up on Tuesday with an "I can't" attitude. Everything felt too hard, including her new summer job at the day care where she worked with two-year-olds. So she decided to call in sick. She did have a monstrous headache, after all.

But her mother didn't give in to that. She said, "Nope. Out of bed. Off to work you go."

So Annabella dragged herself out of bed, took a hot shower, ate breakfast, took something for the headache, and headed off to face her day.

And you know what? Things weren't so bad. In fact, some really cool things happened at work that day. She would have missed them if she'd stayed home. In the end, Annabella was glad she hadn't let the hard stuff keep her away.

You'll have days like that too. Maybe today, in fact! Start by changing your "I can't" to "I can with God's help." Say those words and really mean them in your heart of hearts. He can. No matter how big the problem. No matter how deep the valley. No matter how complicated the mess. He can—and He will, if you don't stop believing.

Keep your hope alive. Don't give up on the "I can't" days. As today's verse says, "Do not let anything stop you from praying." (Hey, that's what the enemy of your soul wants most of all, to disconnect you from God. Don't let him!)

Thank You for reminding me that I don't have to be ruled by my feelings, Jesus. They lie to me a lot. They tell me things are too hard, that I'm not going to make it through. I'm so glad to know that my feelings aren't the boss of me! Amen.

Day 74

How to Love Like Jesus

"A new commandment I give to you, that you love one another: just as I have loved you, you also are to love one another."

JOHN 13:34 ESV

Cassidy loved hanging out with her friends and family. She spent quality time with them whenever she could—laughing, talking, playing games, watching TV, baking cookies, and so much more. She enjoyed every single minute with her loved ones and couldn't get enough. They had so much in common that being with them was super easy. She felt totally comfortable around them, in fact.

If someone had said, "Cassidy, I think you need to branch out and get to know more people," she would have argued with them. "What are you talking about? I'm busy enough! I'm such a people person! Don't you see that?"

But here's the thing: Even though she spent a lot of time with people, they were always the same people. She had a very tight circle. Cassidy was a little—what's the word?—*cliquish.*

After her parents pointed this out to her, she decided to think outside the box and befriend some new people. Oh, she didn't leave the old ones. She just widened her circle to include more girls at school. And a few guys too. She decided to choose the ones that were left out so they would feel included.

That's how Jesus did it, right? He picked the ones who were broken. Lost. Confused. He picked the ones who were sick. He even picked tax collectors (the very people that others didn't want anything to do with). In the end, Cassidy made a ton of new friends and learned a lot in the process.

Jesus has always been a lover of people. *All people.* People of every age, every race, every persuasion. People who love Him back and people who can't stand Him. He loves sinners and saints. He even loves people who think He doesn't exist. (Can you imagine?)

And He wants you to have that same kind of loving attitude toward the people you meet. When you love like that, you make a big difference in this world, girl. And isn't that what you want to do—make a difference for Him?

Love big. That's how Jesus does it.

Show me how to love like You, Jesus.
I want to have a wide circle, one that
makes people feel welcomed and loved.
Give me Your heart, I pray. Amen.

Day 75

To Mentor and Be Mentored

Tell older women to live their lives in a way that shows they are dedicated to God. Tell them not to be gossips or addicted to alcohol, but to be examples of virtue. In this way they will teach young women to show love to their husbands and children.

TITUS 2:3–4 GW

Who mentors you? Who do you mentor?

You might read those questions and say, "Huh? What do you mean?"

The Bible is filled with great stories about people who mentored (poured into the lives of) others. Like Elijah and Elisha. Moses and Joshua. Naomi and Ruth. And, of course, Jesus. He was the greatest mentor of all. He trained the twelve disciples to go on preaching and teaching long after He returned to heaven.

Take a look at today's verse. It was always part of God's plan for women to mentor one another. The older women in your world have a lot to teach you—and not just about housekeeping and child rearing! You can learn from local businesswomen and ministry leaders too. And what about your teachers? No doubt they would be thrilled to mentor you.

And while you're thinking about sharing life skills, don't forget: God wants you to mentor others too. Think of someone in your life who is younger than you—a sibling, neighbor, or girl at church. No doubt she needs someone like you to pour into her life. And it doesn't necessarily have to be someone who is younger in years. Maybe you have a new friend who is young in her faith. She hasn't been a Christian as long as you. If you take the time to mentor her, she'll grow, and so will you.

Zoe was blessed to have a mentor in her life. Her aunt Gail stepped up and taught her a lot of things—but the best was how to sew. Gail was a great seamstress and thought that Zoe might enjoy learning too. So she took the time to pour into her, to teach her many different life skills that would come in handy for years to come. Zoe learned a lot; but more than anything, she developed a real bond with her aunt. And she fell in love with sewing along the way.

That's how it works. You learn. You teach. You share. You love. It's a win-win for all involved!

Thank You for the godly mentors in my life, Jesus. I'm grateful for each one. Now show me how I can pour into the lives of others, I pray. Amen.

Day 76

Put an End to Bullying

Whoever says he is in the light and hates his brother is still in darkness.

1 John 2:9 ESV

Bullying can be in your face or subtle, but it's everywhere these days. It's online (social media). By text. In person. And it's rampant in schools, where teens gather day in and day out. People gang up against someone and think it's funny or cool, but there's nothing funny or cool about it. People get hurt, and sometimes people pay the ultimate price. Kids have been known to commit suicide after being bullied.

So, yeah, not cool. In fact, it's one of many things that surely break God's heart, and He wants it to stop. You can play a role in stopping it, girl.

Sara struggled with being bullied most of her life. She didn't look like the other kids. Born with a facial disfiguration, she struggled to fit in with the crowd. They pushed her out of their circles a lot. And she heard some of the mean things they said behind her back. Sometimes they didn't even wait until her back was turned. They just spit out their ugly words right in front of her.

Many times she wanted to give up. To hide at home. To

pull away from people altogether. But she didn't. She kept trying. Kept going. Kept praying that God would bring just the right friends.

And He did! He sent Nina, a girl who saw past Sara's (supposed) flaws. She was a genuine friend, one who wouldn't let others pull any stunts. She served as a protector, a guardian, and (best of all) a true confidante. And she loved Jesus, so. . .bonus!

Maybe you feel like Sara. People push you aside based on how you look. Or your personality. Or the fact that you're a book nerd instead of a beauty queen. For whatever reason, they've chosen to pick on you. You must stand up and speak up. Tell someone. Don't worry about whether they will get mad at you. It's critical to involve someone who can help. And if you're seeing someone being bullied, don't stand on the sidelines. Take a stand. Let those bullies know that you're not joining them and that their hateful words won't be tolerated.

It starts with one person standing up to the mob mentality. You can be that one person.

Jesus, use me to speak up and speak out against bullying. It breaks my heart to see people hurt, and I know it must break Yours too! I want to make a difference, Lord. Use me, I pray. Amen.

Day 77

The Heavens Declare It!

The heavens declare the glory of God,
and the sky above proclaims his handiwork.

PSALM 19:1 ESV

Everything on the planet is telling the story of God. No kidding! The oceans? They're singing His praise with every crashing wave. The majestic mountain peaks? The snow on top? It's a constant reminder that He's in control of the seasons. The butterflies flitting by? They're a beautiful reminder that God is in the business of growing and changing us. (Hey, if He can take a caterpillar and turn it into a butterfly, He can do anything, right?) Puppies, kittens, lambs, and bunny rabbits? Yep, they're saying, "He made us! Isn't He amazing?"

If you ever begin to doubt the existence of God, just open your eyes, girl! Look at that twinkle in your grandpa's eyes. Check out the dimples on your baby sister's face. Snuggle with your puppy and enjoy his kisses. Spend some time in nature, feeling the breeze against your cheek. Every single thing was created by God and serves as a reminder that He cared enough about us to make sure we had it all.

Luscious foods? He created them. Juicy apples. Yummy chocolate. Spicy peppers. Yep, He made all of that. And He didn't stop there! He made sunsets and rainbows, moonlight, and more galaxies than we can comprehend. He set the stars in the night sky to light our way and gives us the joy of sunlight for the daytime.

On top of everything else, God created humans in His image, to be creative like Him. So we take the things He made (for example, minerals in the earth) and turn them into things like cars and buildings.

It's pretty remarkable if you think about it! We're creative too!

And the heavens are declaring the beauty and glory of God! Don't believe it? Go outside and look up, up, up. Stand there awhile. Really stare at those fluffy clouds in that beautiful blue sky, and just see if you don't feel closer to God.

You will. You can't help but feel closer to the Creator when you spend time in His creation. The heavens are declaring His handiwork even now! How marvelous!

Jesus, I get it! All of nature sings Your praises! Everything points to You—the sun, the moon, the stars, and even the fields of flowers. They all sing, "We were created by the Creator of all!" Thank You for making me creative like You, Lord! Amen.

Day 78

Weighty Matters

The Lord said to him, "Pay no attention to how tall and handsome he is. I have rejected him, because I do not judge as people judge. They look at the outward appearance, but I look at the heart."

1 Samuel 16:7 GNT

Christina struggled with her weight from the time she was a little girl. Her mama always told people that she was a chubby baby, and she had the pictures to prove it. As Christina got older, the pounds kept coming on. She didn't do it on purpose, but it always seemed to be a problem. And when she got to her teens, her size really started to get her down. She tried diets, but they didn't really work. She couldn't seem to stick with them for long. And every time she got depressed about her weight, it just made her want to eat more, anyway. So she did. She hid in her room and ate chips and cookies. Then the number on the scale went up even more!

Lily had the opposite problem. From the time she was young, she was very thin. She could eat anything she wanted and never gain weight. Most girls thought this was great, but she got tired of being called skinny. It bugged her. She just wanted to look "normal." (Is there such a thing?)

Here's the truth—whether you're tall, short, thin, or a little on the fluffy side, you're probably going to find something about yourself to dislike. Most girls struggle with the reflection they see in the mirror. They see pictures of models in magazines and think, *That's what a girl should look like*. And they don't match the picture on the page.

Problem is, that's *not* what most normal girls look like. Girls come in all shapes and sizes, and they're all beautiful. Sure, there are times when you really do have to pay attention to how much food you're eating or how much exercise you're getting. If your health is suffering, you'll really want to stay on top of things. But don't hyper-focus on the image in the mirror, girl. It's not worth it. No matter how many freckles you might have. No matter how chubby your thighs might be. You're still gorgeous, girl!

Thank You for the reminder that I'm beautiful in Your sight, Jesus. I want to be healthy, but I don't want to be so fixated on how I look that I get hung up on it. Help me, please. Amen.

Day 79

Healthy Patterns

Do not be conformed to this world, but be transformed by the renewal of your mind, that by testing you may discern what is the will of God, what is good and acceptable and perfect.

ROMANS 12:2 ESV

A pattern (or a habit) is the way you do something. It shapes who you turn out to be. It molds you into the person you're going to become and helps guide you every step of the way.

Don't believe it? Think about the kind of pattern a seamstress uses. If she chooses a blouse pattern, she's not going to end up with a skirt in the end. If she chooses a Christmas angel costume, she's not going to end up with a ball gown. The pattern determines the result.

So patterns in your life are important. God wants you to develop healthy ones so that you can be strong in every area. Take your eating, for instance. Why does He care so much about your eating patterns? Is God really worried about cellulite on your thighs, or is there something more to this? Truth is, He wants you to be healthy and strong, because He has called you to great and mighty things, girl! That won't be possible if you're dealing with food addictions or stomach issues.

And what about your thought life? If your thought patterns are off (like, if you beat yourself up all the time), you'll never be effective for God. That's one reason He says you should take control of your thoughts, because they too determine your outcome. Happy thoughts, happy outcome.

Another area where it's important to develop healthy patterns is in your relationships. God isn't out to destroy your fun. But if you're hanging out with kids who party—who drink, smoke, or do drugs—then you're more likely to end up doing those things too. He wants you to remain pure, because He knows you will thrive if you do. And thriving is important because, *again,* He has big stuff ahead for you; and you'll need to be in tip-top shape when it all happens.

Healthy patterns are God's best. What good habits do you need to add to your daily routine?

There are lots of great habits I should add, Jesus! My diet could be better. And my sleep patterns. Okay, and my friendships. Hmm. Maybe I should make a list! Thanks for helping me with this, Lord! Amen.

Day 80

Life Skills

But all things should be done decently and in order.

1 Corinthians 14:40 ESV

Bethany felt pretty useless when it came to fixing things. A ripped hem in her jeans? Yeah, she couldn't do anything about that. A missing button on her shirt? Mom would take care of it.

She didn't really tackle cooking, either. When her mother asked her to toss the salad, she passed the job to her sister. And that time she baked a cake for her grandmother's birthday? That was a fiasco. It was a big, fat flop (though her grandmother acted as if it were the best cake she'd ever eaten).

Bethany's parents decided it was time for a few life skills lessons. They made a plan to help her with the basics—managing money, cooking, even changing a tire. Bethany spent months learning all she could about basic things; and by the end of the experiment, she could do almost anything they asked of her. And all of it with a smile on her face. She felt a great sense of accomplishment, especially on the day she helped her dad change the oil in his car. Turned out she was quite the handyman—er, girl. Go figure. Knowing she could tackle new tasks gave Bethany unexpected confidence. Hey, if she could change the oil in a car, what else could she manage? Maybe anything!

Perhaps you read Bethany's story and flinched. No thanks. You'd rather not tackle any of those things, thank you very much. Or maybe you get excited because you're itching to try new things. Well, what's keeping you? As you move into adulthood, you're going to need all sorts of skills. You could start tackling them now and become an expert. Bake that cake. Learn to roll out pie dough. Chop those vegetables. Figure out how to put together a casserole. Load the washer. Discover the joy of prepping your school lunches the night before. Help organize the garage. Use labels in a fun, exciting way in the pantry.

You get the idea. There are all sorts of life skills you can learn now. And guess what? God smiles on all of them. He's all about organization! (Check out today's Bible verse for proof.)

Dive in, girl! There's so much to learn!

I get it, Jesus. I have a lot to learn.
I'm wide open to new ideas. Give me a plan,
and then give me the skills, I pray! Amen.

Day 81

Give Yourself Away

Do not neglect to do good and to share what you have, for such sacrifices are pleasing to God.

HEBREWS 13:16 ESV

Stefani was a giver. If she saw someone in need, she always rushed in to help. That family who didn't have Christmas gifts? She put a plan in motion to gather the items to surprise them. Before long she had a whole team of people shopping and wrapping presents. (Fun, right?) That elderly neighbor who couldn't afford her medicine? Stefani told her parents, and they stepped up to get the prescription filled for her. It made a huge difference in her neighbor's life. That man who always shook her hand at church, the one who told her that he loved chocolate chip cookies? She baked some for him. Then she took the time to visit with him while they ate a couple of them together. Boy, did he enjoy that. She did too!

Stefani's giving didn't stop there. She gave kindness to her teachers. And joy to the people she hung out with. She gave peace to her parents by doing what they asked of her. And she gave gentleness to her siblings by treating them kindly (even when they didn't always deserve it). She gave water to the homeless man on the corner and a kind word to the woman who snapped at her mother in the grocery store. She just kept on giving, no matter what ugly things people tossed her way. And you know what? It changed the atmosphere. It changed that woman at the grocery store. It helped the man on the corner. It brought a smile to the face of the man at church.

Maybe you're thinking, *Wow, that Stefani was something really special*. Here's the deal—you don't have to be a super giver to make a difference in someone's life. Just pay attention. Notice. It's really that simple! What do they need? How can you fill that need? Can you bake cupcakes? Make a meal? Mow a lawn? Sew on a button? Can you send a nice card or letter? Offer a smile? Offer your services to clean their home?

There are thousands of ways to give yourself away, girl. Make up your mind to do so today, and then watch as God changes the atmosphere!

I'll do it, Jesus! I'll give myself away. I want to be a girl who notices others and who cares deeply. Show me how to be a giver like You, Lord! Amen.

Day 82

Which Way Are You Going?

"Have I not commanded you? Be strong and courageous.
Do not be frightened, and do not be dismayed,
for the Lord *your God is with you wherever you go."*

Joshua 1:9 ESV

Jada was terrible with directions. *Really* terrible. She could get lost on her way to places she'd been dozens of times before. And when people said things like "Go south on Frazier Street," she always had to ask, "Now, which way is south, again?" and, "Where's Frazier? Can someone remind me?" Sometimes she even had to look down at her hands to remind herself which was right and which was left. Her friends would laugh and call her "directionally challenged."

Maybe you're directionally challenged too. You could get lost on your way to the bathroom. And when you're out and about, you can't seem to remember how to get from point A to point B, no matter how many times you've made the journey before. Thank goodness for GPS, right?

Sometimes life is a little bit like a journey. You wish you had a map to guide you to the next destination. You're not sure which way to go. Should you join the drama club or the debate team? Should you take biology or anatomy this semester? Should you stay up late and do your homework or get up early and do it in the morning? (Tip: You should probably go ahead and get it over with tonight.)

Decisions have consequences. You know because you've suffered a few already! And you want the road ahead to be as straight and easy as possible. But you know from experience that life isn't always like that.

Here's the cool thing about the Holy Spirit. The Bible calls Him your guide. He's inside of you right now, this very minute, ready to lead and guide you. He gives wisdom. He whispers in your ear, "Do this!" or "Do that!" If you push away the other voices and lean in to hear His, you'll know which way to go. No one will have to tell you. You'll just know in your knower.

He's your map. He's your GPS. And best of all, He's always there. You don't have to go looking for Him. You'll never be lost with God's Spirit leading the way.

Thank You for leading and guiding me, Jesus! I need Your Spirit every minute of every day so that I don't end up going down the wrong path. You'll always lead me in the right direction, and I'm so grateful. Amen.

Day 83

Exposure

Obscene stories, foolish talk, and coarse jokes—these are not for you. Instead, let there be thankfulness to God.

EPHESIANS 5:4 NLT

Noelle wanted to protect her little sister from all of the gross stuff the older kids in the group were talking about, so she sent her out of the room. After all, little ears didn't need to hear such grown-up talk, right?

Then again, neither did she! The kinds of things her friends were talking about were, well, risqué. The conversation started innocently enough, talking about guys. From there, it really got bad. One friend dove into a lengthy story of all the things she and her boyfriend were up to. Gross.

Before long, Noelle wanted to run from the room too. She wanted to protect her own ears and heart. But what could she do? This was her house, after all. She couldn't exactly say, "I need to get home. Mom's waiting on me."

Maybe you've been there. The girls around you are talking, and before long, they're covering topics that make you blush. Then, a few minutes later, the topics are downright disgusting. And there you are, stuck in the middle of it, wondering if you can make an excuse to leave. ("Hey, I need a potty break. See you guys later!")

Truth is, you're exposed to a lot. But you can—and *should*—control how much you allow yourself to hear and see. Don't believe it? Take a look at today's verse. The Bible makes it clear that you're supposed to stay far, far away from obscene (dirty) talk and "coarse" jokes. You know what that means without needing to be told, right? Anyway, when things get uncomfortable (and it happens a lot), you should gather up the courage to walk away. If anyone wants to know why, tell them. If they've crossed a line, they need to know.

And remember, you can stop conversations like that with just a word. Raise your hand and say, "Um, guys, we've gone too far. Let's rein it in." Maybe they're just looking for someone to be accountable. You can be that someone. Jesus will be happy to see you standing up for what's right, and you'll spare yourself the awkward conversation.

I get it, Jesus. I need to step away from not-so-great conversations before they get out of hand. Give me courage in the moment, I pray. I want to make Your heart happy. Amen.

Day 84

The Pursuit of Wisdom

And here's why: God gives out Wisdom free, is plainspoken in Knowledge and Understanding. He's a rich mine of Common Sense for those who live well, a personal bodyguard to the candid and sincere. He keeps his eye on all who live honestly, and pays special attention to his loyally committed ones.

Proverbs 2:6–8 msg

Sabrina was the smartest girl in her circle of friends. If you couldn't figure something out, you could always go to Sabrina. She would know. Everyone assumed she would be the class valedictorian. And for sure she could pick out the college of her choice. No doubt about that. All the smart girls had great futures ahead of them, right?

Only one problem: Sabrina's "smarts" were limited to academics. When it came to choosing a boyfriend? Yeah, not so much. She didn't seem to exhibit the same level of knowledge. And when she had to make a decision about something? She hesitated every time, unsure she could trust her own judgment. Like that time she gave in to the temptation to smoke a cigarette because her friend dared her. Or that time she chose to skip school to hang out at the mall with her BFF.

Yeah, she wasn't the best at making good life choices, but

man, was she great at math problems. And history. And essay writing. That girl was a real whiz academically. Why couldn't it spill over into the rest of her life?

Some people would say that Sabrina had a lot of book smarts but not a ton of godly wisdom. Maybe you know someone like that. They excel in academics, but good life choices, like making decisions about money, for instance? Or figuring out who to hang out with and who to avoid? Not so much.

So what's the difference between knowledge and godly wisdom? Where does wisdom come from, anyway? Is it possible one is acquired by studying and the other comes more naturally, or from someplace altogether different? Take a close look at today's verse. Wisdom (not the same as book smarts) comes straight from the heart of God. He gives it generously. When you draw close to Him, you get it in abundance! That's the key. His wisdom can guide you through the things that worldly knowledge cannot.

You need to be as strong as you can be academically. But hang out with God for hefty doses of wisdom too. Seek both, and you'll go far, girl.

I want to be wise and book smart too. Help me to be the strongest I can be in both areas, Jesus. Amen.

Day 85

Panning for Gold

Good friend, take to heart what I'm telling you;
collect my counsels and guard them with your life.
Tune your ears to the world of Wisdom; set your heart on
a life of Understanding. That's right—if you make Insight
your priority, and won't take no for an answer, searching for
it like a prospector panning for gold, like an adventurer on
a treasure hunt, believe me, before you know it Fear-of-God
will be yours; you'll have come upon the Knowledge of God.

Proverbs 2:1–5 MSG

Jacquie was the daring sort. If someone dared her to do something risky, she wouldn't think twice. She'd dive right in. Several times things did not end well. Like that time she broke her ankle after attempting a drop in on her brother's skateboard. Oh, and the time she decided she would jump across the ditch filled with muddy water. Still, no one could accuse her of being a coward. If someone said, "Go for it!" she did.

The only problem with the "go for it" attitude is that it sometimes spills over into other areas where the danger zone is more problematic. Like experimenting with things that will hurt you. Smoking. Drugs. Cheating. Lying to your parents. Other dangerous behaviors. Things that God never intended for you. When you exhibit risky behaviors with these things, you'll always pay a price in the end. And let's face it, you don't want to end up paying a heavy price. (Ask anyone who is doing time in prison how they feel about their risky behavior now!)

It's one thing to respond to a skateboarding dare, but another to give in to the dare to do something that could change your life forever.

Give today's verse a closer look. There's so much wisdom in these words! If you guard God's counsel (His wisdom, His way) with your life, and if you tune your ears to His Word (His advice) then you'll be wise. You won't be out there like a prospector panning for gold. That might seem like a funny way to put it, but adventure seekers really are like that! They're always looking for the next big thrill. Anyway, if you make God your treasure (the thrill you're seeking), you won't go wrong. In fact, walking with Jesus will be the biggest adventure of your life!

Think about it, girl. Pray about it. What would Jesus chase after? What would thrill His soul? If He wouldn't do it, then you shouldn't either.

I'll chase after You, Jesus. I'll make walking with You the biggest adventure of my life. Curb my appetite for dangerous things, and make me satisfied in You. Amen.

Day 86

A Day Away

You will show me the way of life, granting me the joy of your presence and the pleasures of living with you forever.

Psalm 16:11 NLT

Madeline felt like she needed a break—from everyone and everything. Problems were stacking up—at home, at school, and even with her friends. Ugh. So she asked to visit her cousin who lived in the country. Mom agreed and drove her there to spend the weekend.

When she arrived, Madeline and her relatives went on a picnic at a beautiful lake. It had been ages since she'd eaten outdoors at a picnic table; but even with the ants, she and her relatives had a blast. They even swam in the lake, something she hadn't done since she was a kid.

Afterward, she and her cousin went for a walk down some nature trails. They saw lizards and beetles, caterpillars, and even a garter snake. She loved the smell of the flowers growing along the edge of the trail, and the breeze felt awesome against her skin.

And somehow, seeing—and doing—all of that lifted her spirits. It was a reminder that there was more going on in this great big world than the things she experienced every day in her own little corner of it. More than the work. More than the studies. More than the arguments with Mom. More than the disagreements with friends. More than the constant chaos of trying to keep up with her work, sports, and church life. Just *more*. And she had to step away to find it.

Maybe you're getting a little weary with your corner of the world too. You've forgotten that life exists elsewhere. To you, everything is just the same—day in and day out. You wonder if it will always be like this.

Maybe it's time for a change of pace! Go someplace new for the day. Visit the beach. Drive to a nature preserve. Hang out at a museum and enjoy the artwork. Go to a restaurant you've never been to. Go to the theater. Volunteer at a homeless shelter. Offer to make meals for families in need.

Life is for the living, and there's so much to do. Don't get stuck in a rut. Don't get so bored, so overwhelmed, that you forget the goodness. There's plenty of it out there for a girl like you.

Open my eyes to Your wonders, Lord!
Life is for the living, and I want to live it
to the fullest. Help me, I pray. Amen.

Day 87

I Blew It, but I Won't Quit!

Watch out that you do not lose what we have worked so hard to achieve. Be diligent so that you receive your full reward.

2 JOHN 8 NLT

Jenna worked all summer to prepare for the drill team. The day school started, she signed up for tryouts. And no one was more ready when the day came. She had her cute outfit, her water bottle, and the brightest smile in the room, along with a boatload of confidence. She had practiced all her moves, right down to the tumbling and splits.

But nerves got the best of her, and she ended up kicking the girl next to her by accident. Oh, and then there was that part where she almost slipped and fell. And the part where she pulled a muscle in her leg doing the splits. Ouch!

In all, it was a catastrophic experience, one that left her feeling like a total failure. Not only did she not make the team, but she'd embarrassed herself in the process. Man, talk about a bad day!

Maybe you've been there. You worked really hard at something, but it did not pay off in the end. You really gave it your best shot but were left wondering what more you could have—*should have*—done.

What do you do when life throws those kinds of curveballs at you? In Jenna's case, she thought about quitting. But the following year, she decided to give it another try. She worked out harder, did her best to calm her nerves on the day of the tryouts, and ended up making the team—where she remained until her senior year. In fact, she became captain in the fall of her senior year.

One failure does not a failure make. Read that again. It's so true, girl That failure? It's a hurdle, sure. A life lesson. A bump in the road. But a permanent failure? No way! So keep on trying. Keep on believing. Keep moving forward with confidence. You're learning more about yourself every step of the way, and that's a good thing!

I won't give up, Jesus. Oh, I feel like it. A lot. On the terrible days? Yeah, those really stink! But I'll keep going, even when I'm embarrassed. I'm on a learning curve, but that's okay. You're a great teacher. Most of all, I'm learning not to give up, no matter how hard things get. Thanks for that lesson. Amen.

Day 88

Heaven Is Coming!

We are looking forward to the new heavens and new earth he has promised, a world filled with God's righteousness.

2 PETER 3:13 NLT

Heaven is coming. Don't those words give you hope? When you're facing a terrible situation or feeling all alone, you don't have to fret for long. Know why? Heaven is coming. When someone you love is about to pass away from a lengthy illness, heaven is coming. When the trials of life never seem to end, heaven is coming.

When we get to that amazing place, all of the trials we faced in this lifetime will be a thing of the past. All sickness will be over. All pain will be behind us. (Praise God!) There will be no more heartache, no more tears, no more jealousy, no more anger, no more division, no more strife, no more broken promises.

Heaven will be heavenly. You can count on it! For there, at the very center of it all, will sit the one who loves you most and knows you best—Jesus Himself! You'll spend eternity in a completely different frame of mind than you spent your days on earth. Here you worry and fret over every little thing. Tiny things feel huge. There? Every need will be met, and all worries will be a thing of the past. The only thing you'll focus on is Him. Eternity will be spent praising the one who gave His life for you on the cross. Doesn't that sound amazing?

Take a look at today's verse: "We are looking forward"—we're not staring at the trials of today or the pain of yesterday—"to the new heavens and new earth he has promised." Jesus promised it, and He never goes back on His word! Heaven will be "a world filled with God's righteousness." Right now we live in a broken world. But in heaven, everything will be made 100 percent right and perfect.

Heaven is coming. The next time you're walking through a tough season, just remind yourself, *This is a temporary situation; a better one is on the way.* It really is, you know.

Lord, I'm so grateful for the promise of heaven. I can't wait to see it with my own eyes! I'm so sorry for letting the things of this earth get me down. I'm going to focus on eternal things, Jesus. Help me keep my eyes tilted upward toward heaven. It's coming! Amen.

Day 89

He's Paving a Road

You are the ones chosen by God, chosen for the high calling of priestly work, chosen to be a holy people, God's instruments to do his work and speak out for him, to tell others of the night-and-day difference he made for you—from nothing to something, from rejected to accepted.

1 PETER 2:9–10 MSG

• •

If you've ever watched workers pave a road, you know it's a lot of work. First, they have to dig to form the base. Then they level it out. Then asphalt is poured in sections and left to harden. Finally, lines are painted on the road so that people know exactly where their cars are supposed to go. After the road has passed rigorous inspections, it's ready for traffic. Even then it's not finished. Every few years, it will require maintenance. Lines will need to be repainted. Potholes will need to be filled. It will need tending.

Roads aren't built overnight. It takes a lot of time to get them right. But once they're in place, think of the multiplied thousands of people who can reach their destinations as a result.

God is paving a road in your life right now, at this very moment. He's going to take you places. And, like those workers,

He's not in a hurry. He wants you to learn from Him every step of the way. Sure, going through the paving process isn't easy. He's working in you and through you. Smoothing things out. Digging. Laying new foundations. Giving lines of direction. Adding borders to protect you from harm. But, girl! You're really going places! God has such great plans for you. Don't believe it? Look at today's verse: *You're chosen by God*. Think about that. He picked you. Yes, you! And He has big things for you to do, which is why He is carefully paving the road for you.

And guess what? He's teaching you how to pave roads too. Roads of peace. Roads of love. Roads of forgiveness. Roads of perseverance. So don't fight with Him if things feel off-course right now. Trust Him. He's getting you ready for some amazing adventures, girl!

I trust Your paving process, God. It's not always easy. I feel like You're smoothing out a lot. Sometimes it's painful, rooting out the old, bad stuff and making room for the new. But I trust the process, and I trust You. Amen.

Day 90

You Do You?

I praise you, for I am fearfully and wonderfully made. Wonderful are your works; my soul knows it very well.

Psalm 139:14 ESV

Maybe you've heard the phrase "You do you, Boo." Maybe you've made it your mantra, since you're unique and quirky, different from the rest. That's fine! But remember, just "doing you" isn't always for the best. Sure, it's good to be yourself. But ultimately, you want to be like Christ. "Be like Jesus" might be a better phrase to repeat, because becoming more like Him is the key.

Brittany decided to do an experiment to see if she could become more like Jesus. She memorized the words "Respond like Jesus" and used them in some tough situations.

At school when the girl at the next lunch table started cussing her out.

On the bus when someone refused to let her sit down.

At home when her little brother broke her phone.

At the store when the woman in line behind her got irritated because she was taking too long to check out.

In the kitchen while doing the dishes after dinner.

Her desire to respond like Jesus (instead of her normal

reactions) saved the day in every case. Okay, so not everything was perfect. That girl in the lunchroom had some real issues. But responding in a godly way helped calm the situation. And that lady at the store? She really simmered down when Brittany offered to pay for her items. Even Mom calmed down once the dishes were done. The girl on the bus finally offered her a seat. Oh, and her little brother cried when she told him that she forgave him for breaking her phone. His tears broke her heart.

In other words, responding like Jesus worked for every situation. And it will work for you too. When you respond like Jesus, you're applying ointment to an open wound. It's like medication, meant to heal. And if you think about it, that's what Jesus does best—He fixes broken things, makes things better.

You can make them better too, if you'll live like Him. It's really that simple (and that complicated). So what are you waiting for? Be like Him. It's the only way to be!

I want to be more like You, Jesus! I want my reactions to be Your reactions, my responses to be Your responses, my words to be Your words. Give me Your heart, I pray. Amen.

Day 91

Learning to Love Them All

*"Greater love has no one than this,
that someone lay down his life for his friends."*

John 15:13 ESV

Ashley had a little bit of a "me" problem. Most of her conversations were about herself. When she bragged, it was on her own accomplishments. When she complained, it was always to defend herself. And when she was wrong? Well, let's just say she would never admit it.

Maybe you know someone like Ashley. They're a little hard to be around at times. There you are, in the middle of a conversation about something difficult you're going through, and she interrupts with "Oh, I know. Tell me about it." Then she dives into a conversation about herself.

Sigh.

You want to be kind, but she makes it difficult. She's always turning the spotlight on herself. And you've had enough.

But you still love her. So what do you do?

One way to deal with a person like this is to take them in small doses. Be her friend; but if she's all-consuming, then back away from the fire and only spend small amounts of time with her. If she interrupts, politely say, "As I was saying," and then go back to your conversation. But don't stop loving her. Maybe she just needs a little guidance. (And hey, she might have a completely different personality type than you, one that tends to be a little wordier.)

Of course, the ultimate answer to how to deal with any of your friends is "Be like Jesus." He had all sorts of friends in His circle, and He knew how to deal with them.

Peter was kind of a wishy-washy friend. He had faith to walk on water one minute and was denying Jesus the next. Judas, well, we know about him. He turned his back on Jesus and betrayed Him. James and John were called the "Sons of Thunder." You can imagine what they were like. Matthew was a dishonest tax collector before he turned his back on his old life and started following Jesus. But Jesus somehow managed to love them all.

You'll figure out how to love them all too—even the ones who are very, very different from you.

If You can do it, Jesus, I can try too! My friends don't always make it easy, but I know they are worth it. Show me how to be the best friend I can be and to love as You love. Amen.

Day 92

Haven't Seen It Yet

Jesus said to them, "Have faith in God. For sure, I tell you, a person may say to this mountain, 'Move from here into the sea.' And if he does not doubt, but believes that what he says will be done, it will happen. Because of this, I say to you, whatever you ask for when you pray, have faith that you will receive it. Then you will get it."

MARK 11:22–24 NLV

Callie had a big dream, to make the National Honor Society. By the time she hit eighth grade, she was sure her grades would get her there. But she barely missed out on making it in. So she kept trying. And even though it took longer than she would have hoped, the moment finally came when she got the word that she had made it. Whew!

Here's the thing, though: She saw it long before she "saw" it (if that makes sense). In her mind's eye, she always saw herself making it there. So she had the courage and stamina to move forward, because she already believed it to be true.

What are you seeing? What do you believe to be true about your life journey? It's easier to plow forward when you have confidence that God is going to do something. Having faith builds your courage and helps you keep going, even when things don't seem to be moving in the right direction.

Take a look at today's verse. Jesus wasn't messing around when He said, "If you have faith you can move mountains." He really meant it. Remember, He worked miracles, after all! He had seen a lot.

You might say, "Well, that was Jesus. He's the Son of God. Of course, He had supernatural faith. Of course, He saw miracles." But He clearly wants us to see them too. Otherwise He never would have left us with verses like the one you're reading today. So increase your faith. If there's a mountain standing in your way (fear, doubt, financial problems, anxiety, or anything else), speak to it in the name of Jesus and command it to go. Then step boldly forward, believing with your whole heart that He has great plans for you. He does, you know!

Today I speak to the mountain of ____________________. I tell you that you have to go, in Jesus' name! I believe in faith that God is for me, not against me. No weapon formed against me will prosper. Amen.

Day 93

Modesty, Girl!

Haven't you yet learned that your body is the home of the Holy Spirit God gave you, and that he lives within you? Your own body does not belong to you. For God has bought you with a great price. So use every part of your body to give glory back to God because he owns it.

1 CORINTHIANS 6:19–20 TLB

When you hear the word *modesty*, what comes to mind? Maybe a girl dressed in old lady clothes? Someone wearing a turtleneck sweater or long skirt?

Sure, it's important to dress modestly. We'll talk about that in a moment. But it's also important for Christian girls to *live* modestly—to guard their speech, their actions, and their thoughts. That means you can't go too far with the jokes you tell (or the ones you listen to). It means you need to watch your language. And when you feel like losing your temper, you need to put a lid on it. It means you bring honor to God with all you say and do. (No pressure!)

And, of course, it means you pay close attention to what you wear. But why? Why do you suppose God cares so much about His girls being modest?

Cynthia learned this the hard way. From the time she turned

eleven, she was very shapely. She had curves in places that the other girls did not. And she just got curvier as the years went by. Because she was—as she liked to describe it—"top-heavy," she had to be careful not to wear tight or low-cut tops. Other friends had the cutest clothes, and she often envied them; but every time she tried on a cute T-shirt like the ones they were wearing, well, let's just say the effect wasn't quite the same. So she learned to dress appropriately.

Some girls take advantage of their curves and show off as much skin as they think they can get away with. They draw attention to their bodies every time they can. But this isn't a God-honoring way to live. Sure, it's fine to look cute (and to wear cool clothes), but check your heart and your motivation. If the ultimate goal is to get the guys to check you out? Well, you might want to rethink that outfit. Just saying.

It's not a legalistic kind of thing. This is a matter of the heart, sweet girl. Be modest, because you're a daughter of the one true King. A princess would honor her father with every move she made and every outfit she wore.

I get it, Jesus. I want to honor You, so I'll keep that in mind when I'm choosing my outfits. Amen.

Day 94

The Gift of Community

You are a chosen people, a royal priesthood, a holy nation, God's special possession, that you may declare the praises of him who called you out of darkness into his wonderful light. Once you were not a people, but now you are the people of God; once you had not received mercy, but now you have received mercy.

1 PETER 2:9–10 NIV

Have you ever wondered why people live in communities? Why do we have neighborhoods? School districts? For as long as there have been people, there have been clusters. People like to stick together. Families, extended families, neighborhoods, communities, cities, counties, states, nations—people love hanging around other people with whom they have something in common.

You're no different. You love hanging out with "your people" too. They get you. You get them. And hey, finding someone who "gets" you is pretty important these days. (What a gift!) So enjoy them while you can. Cherish them while you can. And do your best to make sure you're all headed to heaven together so that the fun doesn't have to end when this life is over. (Isn't that the goal, to point people to heaven, after all?

What better place to start than with those you love?)

Jesus had His twelve. You have a tight circle too. And sure, you'll meet lots of people as you get older. But for now, begin to thank God for the ones He's already given you. They are a gift. That kid sister? That rotten older brother? That cousin you go on vacation with? Those parents who sometimes annoy you? That BFF who drives you crazy at times? Those girls you text with? They're your circle. They love you, and you love them (even when you don't always act like it). Your friends from church? Those kids from the youth group or the worship team? Celebrate them! They're such a blessing to you.

Enjoy them all. Pray for them all. Spend time with them all. But remember, there are probably people out there who've been pushed out of circles. They have no one. So make room for them in yours, if you dare. Living like that—loving like that—could very well change a life, and it might even be yours!

I'm so happy to live in community, Jesus. Thank You for surrounding me with amazing, godly people who pour into my life. I don't ever want to take them for granted. They are a gift, and I'm so grateful for them. Amen.

Day 95

Can't We All Get Along?

Know this, my beloved brothers: let every person be quick to hear, slow to speak, slow to anger.

James 1:19 ESV

People these days! They just can't seem to get along, right? Everyone's bickering and arguing over the dumbest stuff. Some of it's not even real. Or it's exaggerated. And worst of all, no one seems to communicate properly. They shoot off a quick, angry text or post an inflammatory social media post meant to take a subtle dig at someone else. But it's not so subtle. People get hurt. Friendships end. And all of it is completely avoidable.

The Lord never intended for us to communicate like this. He always had a way for resolving issues, and it starts with honest, loving conversation. No, it won't be easy. Yes, it will be worth it.

Take a look at today's verse if you want to see His way of doing things:

"Be quick to hear." This means your ears are open before your mouth.

"Slow to speak." Again, your mouth is the last thing to move.

"Slow to anger." So even if you're getting worked up in your heart, you can't blow like a firecracker at every little thing. Always feeling like you have to spout off when you're upset causes more communication problems than anything else.

Take a minute. Cool down. Think rationally. Be sensible. What's going to help the situation long-term? When you do finally speak, your words should be tempered, calm, and rational. This is the only way to keep the conversation from erupting.

You won't always get it right. Neither will your friends. But here's another cool fact: When you're quick to forgive (and quick to admit when you made a mistake), it's like pouring water on a fire. You can put out the flames of anger immediately with these twelve words: "I am sorry. I was wrong. Please forgive me. I love you."

Okay, you might skip the "I love you" part if you're talking to a random kid at school whom you barely know, but you get the idea. You can show love by responding kindly and leading by example.

Lord, I want to have better communication skills, but I'm definitely going to need Your help. I don't want to pop like a firecracker at every little thing. Calm me down, and show me how to speak gently and rationally so that I can be a reflection of You. Amen.

Day 96

Putting Together a Plan

Where there is no vision, the people perish:
but he that keepeth the law, happy is he.

PROVERBS 29:18 KJV

You want to be a good student. In your heart of hearts, you really wish you were more focused on your classes and your grades. But it's hard. Very hard. So many things are tugging at you, and they're so tempting! It's hard to keep your attention on things going on at school. You get a little lost in the swirl of it all.

Natalie really struggled in this area of her life. Her grades were slipping. She felt disappointed and scared. After all, elementary school had been a breeze. And middle school? A little tough, but not like this. Ninth grade was doing her in. She just couldn't keep up with all of her classes. And that homework! It was killing her. Not to mention that last biology test. Ugh. That did not go as expected. But if she confessed that to her parents, they would probably point fingers. They'd say, "Well, then, drop the swim team. It's taking too much of your time and attention." Or "Cut out your hours with your friends and spend more time on your studies."

Those things made sense, but her whole life couldn't be about studying, right? How boring would that be? She would feel totally cheated! And what if they told her to cut out youth group activities? That would really be awful. Surely there was a better way, right?

Let's face it, these are hard things at any age. But if you're struggling to get by at school, it's probably time to talk to a counselor, someone who can help you put together a plan.

Take a look at today's verse: "Where there is no vision [plan], the people perish." Let's just stop right there. Part of the reason people don't succeed is simply because they haven't implemented a plan of action. Without a plan, you're destined to fail, girl. So see a counselor. Put a plan in motion. Then stick with it. Follow the wise advice of someone you trust and, as this verse says, "happy is he"—or, in this case, *she*.

I need a plan, Jesus. Show me who to talk to about all of this. I don't want to panic, but I need to figure out where to go from here. I want to succeed, but I'm definitely going to need help. Point me in the right direction, I pray. Amen.

Day 97

Life's Big Secrets

"This is GOD's Message, the God who made earth,
made it livable and lasting, known everywhere
as GOD: 'Call to me and I will answer you. I'll
tell you marvelous and wondrous things that
you could never figure out on your own.'"

JEREMIAH 33:2–3 MSG

"What's the secret to success?"

"Why do bad things happen to good people?"

"How can I walk with God?"

"How can I know that I'm truly born again?"

Man, these are some deep questions, aren't they? And you want the answers—to all of them. Why not? You deserve the answers.

Gabriella was inquisitive like you. She got hung up on the big stuff—like why God made giraffes' necks so long. And why kids had to go to school. And who decided that days should be twenty-four hours long and years should be 365 days. She spent hours researching things like "Why are oceans salty but lakes are not?" and "How can I get a watermelon to grow from a watermelon seed?"

She was definitely a question-asking girl. And sure, she found a lot of answers online. But when it came to the big stuff? The God questions? The internet couldn't give her the answers she was looking for. No, for those she actually had to spend time with Jesus, to draw close to Him and pray. She had to crack open her Bible and read, read, read to get to the answers she was looking for.

In the end, she found the answers.

The secret to success is in loving God.

Bad things happen because we live in a fallen world.

You can know that you're truly born again simply by praying, "Jesus, come live in my heart. Be my Lord and Savior. I give my life to You."

You can walk with God by simply living the way Jesus lived and loving the way Jesus loved.

Sure, there are questions by the millions. But in the end, the only real answer is found in Him.

Jesus, the answer to all of life's problems is You. I'm so glad I came to know You. I'm so glad I gave my heart and life to You. Thank You for washing me clean and making me brand-new. And thanks for revealing Yourself to me so that I can know the answers to so many of life's puzzling questions. Though I'm still a little curious about that giraffe. Amen.

Day 98

Hey, You Could Always Praise!

Why are you down in the dumps, dear soul? Why are you crying the blues? Fix my eyes on God—soon I'll be praising again. He puts a smile on my face. He's my God.

PSALM 42:11 MSG

You're going through a hard time. Everyone who knows you can see it. You couldn't hide it if you tried. Not that you feel like trying! After all you've been through, you've earned the right to cry, and so you do. The tears flow like rain.

And then a gentle whisper from the Holy Spirit reminds you that you were created for more than the pain you're feeling. You were designed to praise, even in the middle of the darkest situations. No, it doesn't make sense. Yet it feels so right.

So you lift your head. You tilt your face toward heaven and cry out, "I don't get it, God, but I choose to praise You anyway!" Maybe others will think you've lost your mind, but you don't care. Praising your way through the storm is the way to go.

The pain doesn't go away, at least not completely. But over a period of time, as you praise your way through, tiny snatches of it slip away. And the power that comes from praise gives you strength to keep going, no matter how rocky the path ahead.

Justina learned this lesson during a particularly painful season. Her mother was diagnosed with breast cancer and had to go through chemotherapy. Things were okay for a while, and then they weren't. Her mother got so sick that Justina thought she might not make it. During the darkest moments, she wanted to give up, but God wouldn't let her. This message of praise resonated in her heart, and she decided to give it a try. It started small—just a few words like "Jesus, I praise You in spite of the storm we're going through." Soon she was able to praise bigger, louder, and longer. And by the time her mother rang that bell, announcing to the world that she was done with her chemo for good, Justina was ready to give a loud shout of praise.

No matter what you're going through, praise is definitely the answer. So lift your heart, your eyes, and your voice to heaven and begin to thank Him even now.

Lord, I praise You today. Things in my life aren't perfect. There are problems galore. But that won't stop my praise. I'll power my way through with Your help! Amen.

Day 99

The Road to Success

Good friend, don't forget all I've taught you; take to heart my commands. They'll help you live a long, long time, a long life lived full and well. Don't lose your grip on Love and Loyalty. Tie them around your neck; carve their initials on your heart. Earn a reputation for living well in God's eyes and the eyes of the people.

PROVERBS 3:1–4 MSG

Adeline was a girl with a plan. She would be successful at everything she put her hand to. If she tried it, she would conquer it.

Academics. The arts. Sports. There was nothing that girl couldn't do. For years, everyone called her the golden girl. Everything she touched turned to gold. Every sport she attempted ended in a win. Every song she sang sounded good. In short, Adeline could do no wrong.

Until she tried learning French. Suddenly, she got stuck. She just couldn't seem to remember one word from the next. And the harder she tried, the worse she got. Unaccustomed to failure, she didn't know what to do.

She hated to give up, but in the end, Adeline had to admit, "French just isn't for me." The next semester she signed up for the debate club instead and ended up excelling. Turned out she was good at arguing. Who knew?

Maybe you can relate to Adeline's journey. Well, maybe not the "great at everything" part, but the part where she stunk at French. Maybe you've tried things that didn't work and you felt like giving up.

Hey, let's face it—not everyone is good at everything. And, honestly? Who has time to be good at everything? Pick and choose the things that make sense to you, girl. Otherwise, you'll get consumed. (And let's be honest—there are a ton of things you'd probably be pretty good at. No doubt you've already tried a lot of them!)

Does this mean you quit the French class if it's hard? Nope. But be logical. Sign up for something else next time, something that makes more sense. And allow yourself to have fun along the way. Life is an adventure, after all!

I'm not one to give up, Lord, but some things really just aren't for me. Give me the wisdom to know when to move forward and when to try something new. I'm ready for whatever adventures You have in store for me. Amen.

Day 100

God's Not Done with You

"For I know the plans I have for you," says the Lord, "plans for well-being and not for trouble, to give you a future and a hope. Then you will call upon Me and come and pray to Me, and I will listen to you. You will look for Me and find Me, when you look for Me with all your heart. I will be found by you," says the Lord. "And I will bring you back and gather you from all the nations and all the places where I have made you go," says the Lord. "I will bring you back to the place from where I sent you away."

Jeremiah 29:11–14 NLV

God's not done with you.

Go ahead and read those words again. They're so impor tant: *God's not done with you.* In fact, He's just getting started.

Sure, you might feel like things are at a standstill, like your life is going nowhere; but nothing could be further from the truth. You're learning. You're growing. You're getting stronger in your faith. And you're figuring out what it means to love Jesus with your whole heart.

When you're convinced in your heart of hearts that great things are coming, you have what's called a forward-looking attitude. That means you're not too hung up on the negative things happening today. They'll pass. You know they will. You're ready for a bright future; and if you let yourself get too stuck in the quicksand of today's problems, you'll never get there.

So, as Elsa sang, "Let it go." Let go of the mistakes of yesterday. Let go of the worries of today. Grab hold of the faith that says, "Tomorrow is going to be great."

Because it is, you know. It *really* is.

And remember: God promises in His Word that His plans for you go above and beyond anything you could imagine or dream up for yourself. And He's in this for the long haul. He wants to carry those plans all the way through to their completion. So lean on today's verse. Call on Him. Pray to Him. He's listening to you, even now. (No, really! His ear is inclined toward you at this very moment!) He has your best interests at heart and is giddy with delight over the things He has in store. So stick with Him, girl. He adores you.

Jesus, I trust Your great plans for me. I can't wait to see how my life turns out. I don't know where You'll take me, who I'll meet, or what I'll be when I'm grown up, but I know one thing: I'll walk with You every step of the way.

Scripture Index

OLD TESTAMENT

NEW TESTAMENT